# PARENT IN CRISIS

## Finding Peace and Purpose in a Special Needs Home

*John E. Goralski*

A HiJack Publishing Company L.L.C. Book
CONNECTICUT - 2023

Parent in Crisis: Finding Peace and Purpose in a Special Needs Home
Copyright © 2023 by John Goralski
A HiJack Publishing Company L.L.C. Book

All rights reserved. No part of this book may be reproduced in any form or by an electronic or mechanical means, including information storage and retrieval systems, without written permission of the copyright owner, except for the use of quotations used in a book review.

The events and conversations in this book have been set down to the best of the author's ability, although some names and details have been changed to protect the privacy of individuals.

Sale of this book without a front cover may be unauthorized. If this book is coverless, it may have been reported to the publisher as "unsold or destroyed" and neither the author nor the publisher may have received payment for it.

Library of Congress Control Number: 2023915100

ISBN 979-8-9889015-0-1 (hardcover with jacket)
ISBN 979-8-9889015-1-8 (hardcover)
ISBN 979-8-9889015-2-5 (ebook)

First hardcover edition September, 2023

*Book cover by John Goralski*

Published by HiJack Publishing Company L.L.C.
www.JohnGoralski.com

# Contents

## *Parent in Crisis:*
### *Finding Peace and Purpose in a Special Needs Home*

CHAPTER
ONE .......... The Good, the Bad, and the Ugly ........................................1
TWO .......... Crisis? What Crisis? ................................................................ 28
THREE ..... The Balancing Act: Underlying Issues ............................... 49
FOUR ........ Safety and Security: What Worries You, Masters You .... 78
FIVE .......... Social Studies: Can't We All Just Get Along? .................. 106
SIX ............. The Scorecard: Plans, Expectations, and Routines......... 134
SEVEN ..... Dysfunction Junction: Divorce and Separation .............. 153
EIGHT ...... The Speak-Easy: Communication and Language ........... 176
NINE.......... Life Events: Vacation, Death, and Love ......................... 195
TEN ........... Surviving the -ists: Schools and Support Groups ......... 223
ELEVEN .. Let the Good Times Roll: Overcoming the Ordeal ...... 245

APPENDIX
ONE .......... ABOUT THE AUTHOR .................................................. 269
TWO .......... ABOUT THE COVER ..................................................... 271

# CHAPTER ONE

*The Good, the Bad, and the Ugly*

---

I don't think I will ever forget the sound of my son's screams. There are few things I remember more vividly about those early years before he was diagnosed with his condition. Everything else sort of blurs together in a hazy nightmare. Of course, I remember the feelings—the fear, anxiety, guilt, loneliness, and anger punctuated by fits of panic, frustration, and self-pity—but those screams play over every memory like the world's worst soundtrack. It was inescapable, relentless, and the one thread that tied each garbled memory together. On most days, it overwhelmed me.

Calling the sound a scream isn't really doing it justice. It was more like a shriek that punched its way into every corner of our two-room apartment, building pressure like a balloon about to pop. The piercing sound stabbed right through me. It battered me from every side. It drove my thoughts, my words, and my actions. I lived in constant dread of the next screaming tantrum, so I would do anything to avoid it. Every day, our home was transformed into a battlefield as fear of the next bout clouded the time between meltdowns. Sometimes, his fits would erupt suddenly with no warning. Other times, his emotions would simmer slowly to a boil. When the tantrum finally struck, it was impossible to ignore, and those eruptions were the best indication that something was truly wrong with him.

I endured his tantrums for years. Sometimes they turned physical. Sometimes they posed a danger to both him and me, but they always included that bloodcurdling scream. His fits continued long after doctors settled on a diagnosis. They transformed with every new stage of his development, and they dominated our lives in the early years of his condition. Those memories still haunt me.

Public outbursts often drew a crowd, and the looks of judgment and pity were hard to miss. Those looks were even harder to stomach when they came from friends and family. My son and I were often locked in safehold wrestling matches—father versus toddler—at the most inopportune times and places. Attempts to buy groceries often ended with abandoned shopping carts. Events with friends and family usually ended in early exits.

No two tantrums were alike, but there's one that stands out in my memory. This particular event began on the foul line of a youth baseball tournament that I was covering for a small, community newspaper. This was a weekend assignment featuring

## THE GOOD, THE BAD, AND THE UGLY

dozens of baseball games and family activities. As a sports writer and photographer, I was responsible for the story, the interviews, and all of the pictures from the event.

Early on the first day, my toddler was napping behind me in his stroller while I wheeled about my camera. It was a beautiful summer morning, and the air was filled with the sounds of baseball. I clicked away on my camera while my son slept comfortably behind me.

Around the fourth inning, I began to hear him rustling. Within a few minutes, he was fidgeting uncomfortably. His behavior wasn't out of control, but as his fussing continued I could already feel the questioning looks from the parents in the stands. Who was this photographer with a baby at a baseball game? Having taken enough photos for the story, I called it a day. The interviews could wait until the next rounds of the tournament, and it was too early to compile any results. So I gathered my gear and quickly escaped the field.

By the time we reached our car, my son was thrashing about. As we pulled out of the parking lot, he began to cry. We lived just a few miles away, but as we turned onto our street his sobbing transformed into a wail. By the time we turned into our parking space, he was well on his way to a full-blown tantrum. Just as we stepped across the threshold into our apartment, the screaming began ...

Over the next few hours, I fought against the tantrum with

every tool in my arsenal. I fed him. I changed him. I drew the shades in his room, and I tried to comfort him on his bed. But the shrieking continued. I rocked him in my arms, tried massaging his joints, and sang softly in the darkened room. The screams never wavered. He ignored the deep breathing exercises. He began to fight off the hugs. Lullabies weren't working, and he became impossible to soothe. The only thing that didn't change was the screaming. If anything, it grew louder.

As the fit wore on, my patience began to fail me. My neighbors had yet to complain, but I could picture them frustrated by the muffled screams through our paper-thin walls. Should I turn on some music, or would that just add to the noise? Worry turned to frustration. Anxiety turned to anger. Fatigue began to settle in, but the screams continued. At this stage, my goal had shifted from comforting my child to stopping the tantrum at all costs. It's a subtle shift that happens the longer a parent and child are locked in a tantrum. I was no longer concerned about his needs or his state of mind. I was only focused on mine.

We were locked in a head-to-head battle. I screamed back at him, nose to nose, to try to shock him into sanity. I made threats and desperate pleas that he couldn't even understand. At one point, I stormed out of the room and slammed the door, threatening to leave. Of course these manipulative arguments didn't work. How could they possibly work with a child who has limited language skills? But at this point of the ordeal, I wasn't thinking straight. My strategies made perfect sense to me. I can't imagine how that must have seemed to him. With every stage of his tantrum, my behavior became more erratic as I engaged in a fight-or-flight battle with my own child. Every effort to calm him failed. I was bloodied and bruised, but his tantrum continued. So did mine.

Still, his screams continued.

Eventually, the tantrum turned physical, and I spent the next hour fending off his attacks. He clawed at my face. He hit me with his fists and feet, and his attacks were relentless. It always surprised me how strong a toddler can be when anger turns to rage. Self-defense became a full-time effort, and I was getting tired—physically and emotionally—yet I kept fighting off his punches and kicks until they beat me into a state of desperation.

Finally, I surrendered. I still remember that overwhelming feeling of guilt and uselessness as I closed the door behind me, hoping that he'd tire himself out in the dark. I stumbled down the stairs to my living room, but I didn't even make it to the couch. I barely reached the coffee table where I sat with my head in my hands, engulfed by his screams. Totally defeated, I stared hopefully at the door, praying for the hard knock from police that might bring an end to the ordeal. Had someone seen me through my window, it would have been hard to figure out why I was doing nothing about my screaming child. Had someone witnessed my behavior, they might have stepped in to stop it. They might have called some authority to remove my son from my care. In that moment, I probably would have welcomed it.

I was exhausted and angry. I was completely detached from his suffering and deaf to his screams. I no longer cared how long his tantrum continued. I can't remember how much longer it took before his tantrum began to lose its steam because I had already lost mine. At some point it stopped, and my son fell asleep. At some point I fell asleep, too. I never made it into my bedroom. I woke before dawn, still dressed on the couch, and trudged upstairs for a few more moments of rest before the alarm signaled another day. Thankfully, the screaming had stopped ... for now.

My case isn't unique, and this incident wasn't even his worst. Battles like these can be common occurrences in special needs homes—especially at the start of the journey. Sometimes they might stem from some sort of precipitating event, but they often seem to explode out of nowhere—like this one. There was nothing about the baseball game or the beautiful morning that could explain the tantrum that followed. No matter how many times I've replayed it in my mind, I still can't figure out what sparked his crisis.

Most of the time, I could outlast him. Sometimes, my efforts would calm him. Occasionally, I could step in and make a difference, but there were just as many failures as successes. There were times when I would overreact, and others when I would just shut down. There were even frequent temper tantrums from me. When I reacted poorly, the episode was always followed by some sort of emotional hangover. For hours afterward—and even days—I would be tormented by feelings of guilt, self-pity, and inadequacy. Sometimes the hangover was interrupted by the next outbreak, and the process started all over again.

On the other hand, this particular screaming incident marked a turning point for me. By now, it was clear to everyone that my son was struggling with his developmental crisis. We had already begun the long journey from doctors and specialists to preschool teachers and psychologists. There was no question that my son was in crisis as we fought to understand his condition, but this particular tantrum marked the first time I realized that *I was in crisis, too.*

I could try to pretend I had everything under control. In fact, I often portrayed myself as a calm and collected father when I was out in public. I had already developed a reputation among my friends and family for my patience and tolerance, but the reality was that there was a storm raging inside of me as I tried to manage my son's difficulties. I felt like a fraud because I was clearly struggling as much as he was. I was in a perpetual state of stress. I was carrying the weight of the world on my shoulders. I was constantly out of balance. I seemed to be in conflict with everyone and everything—including myself. I was usually annoyed, full of fear, and ready to explode at any point. There were moments of crisis that I couldn't hide, but there was a constant state of crisis just below the surface. My life was spinning out of control.

I didn't talk about my problems because I was sure that nobody else would understand them. How could they when I didn't understand them myself? Fears about my son's condition were compounded by the growing uncertainty in my own life. Confusion, anger, anxiety, guilt, and worry dominated my thoughts. My work was suffering. My personal life was in tatters, and I dreaded any sort of event outside the home. On the rare occasion that I did reach out to family or friends, their responses were always filled with unsolicited advice that just drove home the point that they didn't understand our problems.

Like most special needs families at this stage, I was isolated and depressed. But asking for help was still difficult because of fears about what people would find—with my son, with me, or with our living conditions. Underlying everything was the fear that people would judge me, and I'd lose my son. Despite all of our struggles, challenges, and frustrations, my love for him was as deep as any parent's love for their children, so the fear of losing him was very real to me. It pushed me even deeper into isolation.

This was supposed to be the phase in a child's life where his language was blossoming. The world was supposed to be coming into focus, but my son was lagging way behind the curve. He couldn't ask for food if he was hungry. He couldn't ask for toys, for comfort, or even for his parents. His confusion manifested in fits of anger and frustration. My son was clearly in crisis, and that was heartbreaking.

## THE GOOD, THE BAD, AND THE UGLY

The truth is that I was perpetually on the brink of some sort of emotional crisis, too. Whenever the tipping point came, I was often at my worst. I could be loving and tolerant for very long stretches, only to have it evaporate in an instant. I could be self-sacrificing and patient through all sorts of trials, only to lose control over something trivial. I could devote hours of the day to his needs. I could balance extraordinary pressures with work duties and my family life. I could demonstrate countless examples of poise and dignity for days on end, only to have it come crashing down in a moment of weakness. It didn't seem to make any sense. I could handle something easily, multiple times, for long periods of time. Then, out of nowhere, I'd suddenly shift into a sort of self-defense mode over something unimportant. At my best, I was unpredictable—even to me. At my worst, I was selfish, unloving, and controlling.

It didn't start out like this.

When my son was born, I was earning a good living, enjoying a happy marriage, and experiencing the excitement that comes with a first child. He was born within a month of two close cousins, and at first it seemed that everything was normal despite a rough birth and some early physical issues.

In my mind, there was a healthy competition between my son and his cousins as the three of them were hitting those early milestones. At the time, I enjoyed the unfounded pride that came as my son led the race. He was the first to hold his head up, the first to push himself around with his arms and legs, and the first to hold toys. He was the first to roll over, and the first to sit up on his own. At nine months, he had already begun walking and climbing, while his two young cousins were just beginning to crawl. Even though some special needs parents face struggles right from the start, my experience during those first few months was fairly normal. The future looked bright.

But as advanced as he was with those physical milestones, that doesn't paint the full picture. While his cousins were smiling at their parents, pointing out things in their cribs, and fiddling around with toys and stuffed animals, my son wasn't showing any interest in the world around him. While his cousins were cooing and babbling, he was sitting silently for long stretches of time with an attention span that would rival any adult. It soon became apparent that these were symptoms of some larger issue. As his cousins were piecing together sounds on their way to their first words, my son began alternating between two extremes—silence and screaming.

He was struggling to communicate, making slow progress toward language, and losing those hard-fought skills almost instantly. He had trouble fixating on people, toys, and objects, and he began to repeat behaviors that were unhelpful and abnormal. Social situations brought high levels of stress, and he rarely engaged with other people. He had no interest in other children, playing games, or interacting. He resisted any change to his environment or his routines. My early confidence began to melt away, replaced by feelings of anxiety and jealousy.

I wasn't a bad parent, but I didn't feel like a good one, either. I was fortunate to have good role models because I grew up in a household built by honest and self-sacrificing parents. They weren't controlling or limiting, and they fostered an independence with their children. They allowed us to make mistakes, learn from them, and grow. They didn't take our sides automatically when troubles arose in the backyard, on the school bus, or in the classroom, but they made us accountable for our part in any disagreement. They didn't always defend us blindly when fights arose, but they always seemed to have our backs when it was necessary. They weren't perfect, but even in their worst moments there was no question that I was loved. Through their examples, I forged my own ideal about parenting, but in my own family that perfect ideal often felt out of reach—especially in those moments of stress and confusion.

As my son's special needs began to manifest, I began to stray more and more from my perfect ideal. It was subtle at first. Someone would ask about his progress, and I would lie for no reason. Later, I would worry and fret, while I second-guessed every decision I made. The more he fell behind, the more I threw myself into fixing his problems. I began to hover over him, instructing him constantly, and redirecting him at every turn. With good intentions, I began to instruct and redirect anyone who stepped into our circle. I'd act as interpreter, intermediary, and judge for anyone who came close to us. But the more I tried to control our environment, the more it spun out of control. Over time, I began to develop complex schemes to head off his tantrums before they started. I began to structure his environment with an almost military precision. My sole aim was to keep him happy, well rested, well-fed, and entertained, so that he might avoid another relapse into screaming, punching, and scratching.

My efforts seemed to be supported by everything I read and everything I was told. But, more and more, my efforts at structure were met by my son's rebellion. The more we depended on routine, the less either one of us seemed to be able to handle change or interruptions.

Our peaceful household was beginning to show its cracks. My son's peace of mind was the first casualty, and his parents weren't too far behind him. Without language skills, my son's frustration grew. Temper tantrums became commonplace. They appeared quickly and lasted for hours. Irritation and fatigue spread like a disease throughout our once happy home, and it began to chip away at our marriage. In the beginning, we were a united front. But as our child's struggles continued, we began to grow apart. Competitions emerged over parenting styles, problem-solving strategies, and philosophies about our future. Power struggles and disagreements appeared as the stress level increased. Our home life became a competition that nobody was winning, and the more I tried, the more I struggled.

# THE GOOD, THE BAD, AND THE UGLY

The isolation was overwhelming. I felt trapped in my apartment because leaving was so difficult. Just a simple trip to the grocery store required extraordinary preparation. Even at family gatherings, I was forced to leave early when his inevitable tantrum would erupt. It was hard to take walks in the neighborhood, visit with friends, or find a sitter who was willing or able to handle his needs. I felt like a prisoner and a bad parent. I know that many parents feel this way at times, but it takes on a whole different level in special needs families.

My son began to get referrals for developmental specialists, speech experts, and psychologists as we were hurtled down that frightening path toward a diagnosis. They tested his hearing. They measured his reactions. During a scary two- or three-year journey, experts tested just about everything, and the whole process took on a strange momentum. Occasional victories were followed by even bigger setbacks. Symptoms were ruled out or discovered. Three- and four-syllable words introduced by doctors became more common than my son's attempts at first words or simple sentences. It took a trip to our state capital to have a specialist finally settle on a diagnosis. When I heard the word autism, it sparked a whole other round of doctors and psychologists—and a whole new set of worries, resentments, and anxieties for me.

His diagnosis opened up a world of assistance as my son began to get the support he needed. But as they descended upon our home, it made me feel even more insecure, isolated, and useless. Of course, it felt selfish to think that my needs were just as important as his, but they were. I couldn't sleep. I was constantly in a state of worry, and I was feeling more and more isolated from my friends, my family, and even my son's mother. I'm sure she felt the same way.

By the time my son turned three, our lives had completely transformed. My marriage had crumbled, and one struggling household was suddenly split into two dysfunctional homes. My lucrative insurance career collapsed, replaced by a low-paying job at a local newspaper. Despite my college degree, I was earning little more than minimum wage because our family needed flexibility even more than we needed financial stability. My son and I were living in low-income housing, and I was still struggling to pay our bills. My self-esteem was shattered, and I felt trapped. Every day was the same. Get him on the bus, get as much writing done as possible, drag him to newspaper assignments, feed him, wash him, get him to bed, and finish working until bedtime. The next day, we'd get up and do it all over again.

My son's tantrums began to manifest differently in each environment—in each home, in school, in public and in private. Meltdowns were most common during transitions. Any time he was getting on and off the bus there was a good chance for bad behavior. Whenever he was getting handed off from one parent to the other, he was prone to behavioral problems. He was always on the verge of crisis, and so was I. We were exhausted, barely getting

## THE GOOD, THE BAD, AND THE UGLY

by, and I was constantly worried about the future. It was taking every ounce of energy to balance a seven-day workweek with the demands of my son's special needs, and I was struggling in every aspect of my life. That was my state of mind when I arrived at that youth baseball tournament on a beautiful Saturday morning …

My experience isn't unique, but I really felt like nobody understood what we were going through. Even when I came across specialists, they didn't seem to understand the full picture. Sometimes, the doctors themselves seemed confused. For the first decade of his life, my son's condition was being reworked and ironed out in the medical community as we were trying to get a handle on what it meant to us. Eventually, a diagnosis within a spectrum of disorders merged into an umbrella term for all of them. Different conditions like autism, Asperger's syndrome, and pervasive developmental disorder were merged into one diagnosis. Other conditions, like Rett syndrome and Tourette syndrome, were removed from the spectrum. Sometimes, it seemed that the doctors, themselves, were confused and contradicting each other. It was a confusing time for all of us.

The feeling that nobody understood our unique conditions was made worse when I encountered other parents of special needs children. To me, they always seemed calm and peaceful while I was struggling to hold everything together. So in public I'd play the calm, collected parent, and at home I'd give in to the chaos. This is fairly common in special needs homes. Many parents become great stage actors, playing one role for outsiders and another in our homes. Of course, this often leads to more confusion and more isolation. It certainly did with me.

Homes with special needs children are often stressed to the breaking point. Even when marriages survive, there can be no shortage of dysfunction in a family. It can be even more complicated if there are siblings who feel pushed to the side as the special needs child necessarily gets more attention and care. Homes become battlegrounds, and families become isolated from the outside world—and each other. It is a very lonely existence.

These days, I've learned to spot a special needs parent in public. After all, it takes one to know one. If I look closely, I can recognize that physical and emotional fatigue that I used to see etched across my face in the mirror. These parents can sometimes seem like they are totally disconnected from the society around them, losing tempers in mid-sentence or at inappropriate moments. They might seem to have split personalities—calm and patient in one moment but disheveled and emotional in the next. Lives get put on hold or diverted. Careers get sidelined. Relationships dissolve.

A parent's whole sense of self begins to get wrapped up in the perception of family, friends, and complete strangers as they try to hold everything together perfectly. We build a house of cards around us that's ready to come tumbling down in the slightest breeze. We get wrapped up in schemes for even the simplest tasks

# THE GOOD, THE BAD, AND THE UGLY

such as a family gathering or a trip to the store. Feeling like an outsider trapped in the spotlight waiting for the other shoe to fall … always on the edge of crisis … then it inevitably hits.

The sad part is that many parents in a special needs household don't even realize that they are in crisis. The out-of-control life almost seems normal. That's why I'm so grateful for that daylong ordeal after the baseball game and that momentary revelation that I was in crisis, too. It might have been obvious to others, but it came to me like an epiphany. It forced me to confront the truth about myself—that these moments of crisis were more commonplace than I cared to admit.

I used to think that I was good in a crisis, but I was really just used to being in crisis. It's easy to think that some people—firefighters, police officers, or EMTs—are good in a crisis. After all, these people rush into situations that most people run away from, but the reason that they are able to be so calm under pressure is because of their training and the discipline that it brings. When firefighters race into a burning building, it's not a crisis for them. When a police officer successfully de-escalates a chaotic situation or an EMT stays calm in a life-threatening situation, it's because they rely on their training. I'm sure that when these very same people are panicked or angry—at work or at home—they react much like everyone else. Nobody is good in an emotional crisis.

It became easy to see that, if I was going to survive my daily living with some measure of grace and dignity, I would have to be better trained at avoiding those moments of crisis. I had to do much more than just identify them after they erupted. I had to be proactive. I had to understand how the crisis builds within me and learn to solve those underlying conditions before they took hold of me.

I began to look for examples of crisis in my daily life. It almost became a game as I tried to spot those emotional spikes throughout my day. Sometimes, they were huge meltdowns or tantrums. Often, they manifested in anxiety or annoyance. There was a whole spectrum of feelings and behaviors that could be classified as "moments of crisis," but there wasn't a day that went by where I couldn't identify at least one. On most days, there were several.

The more I reviewed my life, the more I began to notice that I was often on the brink of some sort of catastrophe. With a certain amount of discipline, I became better at proactively avoiding my meltdowns. Over time, I even became skilled at seeing them develop in my son—before he reached his tipping point. That was another real turning point in our household. For the first time since his special needs began to manifest, I could identify with him. I wasn't any closer to becoming an expert on his condition—and I'm still not—but I began to develop expertise with the resulting behavioral problems. His and mine. Recognizing that we were both struggling with our behaviors was like striking gold. I could finally see that we were both competing to get our way, and neither of us

# THE GOOD, THE BAD, AND THE UGLY

was ever really getting it.

He was special. I was not. But we did have common emotional problems. Finding a solution to those problems was critical for both of us. If I could learn to recognize the causes and conditions that led to my crisis, I might be able to avoid it. If I could learn to recognize these same conditions in my son, I might be able to help him to understand his feelings and grow. In fact, we both might be able to avoid those meltdowns entirely. At the very least, with a better understanding and better coping skills, we could lessen the emotional impact. Best of all, we could do it together.

I began to see that it wasn't the people or events that were my problem. It wasn't even my son or his troubles. I began to see how I was letting people or circumstances push my buttons. More importantly, I began to understand those buttons, themselves. Some buttons seemed to get pressed constantly. My anxiety would build up to a tipping point, and I would finally react. I could usually handle the first incident. Sometimes, I could handle the second, but at some point some poor button-presser would prove to be too much. I felt sorry for that person who put me over the edge. Either they would face retaliation for everyone and everything that came before them, or I would turn it inward on myself. More often than not, the person in the crosshairs when that tipping point came was my own child—the one who needed me the most.

As I became more aware of these "buttons," I began to see them in people around me—including my son. Learning to deal with them myself put me in a better position to help him deal with the button-pressers in his own life—even me. While he didn't have the language or ability to understand these problems, I found that my knowledge of myself, along with my experience, helped us to make sense of his problems. I learned ways to communicate and developed better ways to coach him through his own feelings.

Most importantly, he could finally learn from his parent. I began talking about my successes and failures in a way that helped us both. Even though his language was still very limited, talking about my problems seemed to help us both. Our discussions became more focused on the buttons and less focused on controlling outbursts. Even when he was very young and his language skills were very limited, we both seemed to respond to this approach. As I shared my experiences, it was almost as if I was putting his own feelings into words. Even though he probably didn't understand it all, the approach seemed to work. We both began to experience real change with a true sense of calm. It didn't solve all of those moments of crisis, but it did make them more rare and less severe.

The greatest change is that I finally began to live up to my ideals about parenting. My intentions were always good, but my actions finally began to line up with them. I learned how to be self-sacrificing without self-pity. I learned how to be honest about my limitations, while learning to recognize my strengths. I found that I was able to let go of most of my fears and allow my son to make his own mistakes, learn from them, and grow. I didn't have to battle everybody and everything, and in the process I became a better advocate for his needs. I became a better partner with the experts who were trying to help my son, and a better partner with his mother. I became less controlling, less self-centered, and more peaceful.

That tranquility went beyond our family life, spilling into every aspect of my work life and personal life. Our home was no longer a battlefield. It was our sanctuary, and we both began to thrive. In a very real sense, we began to grow up together. In fact, most healthy families do. Even without special needs children, most parents are flying blind in those early stages of parenting until we learn ways to cope with our unique circumstances. That's the true legacy that we pass on to our children, and everyone grows from the experience until children become adults, themselves. This maturing process is even more important in special needs households where plans, security, and social challenges pose even greater obstacles for the child—and the parent.

We aren't perfect. My son still has his troubles, but those moments that end in crisis are fewer. I still have days when I'm emotional, angry, or filled with fear, but it has been years since I've battled my son during his meltdowns or withdrew when he needed me the most. Each of us still has bad days, but it's rare when we are both having a bad day at the same time. That is a monumental change from those early days of crisis.

Life still presents hurdles to overcome, and it can sometimes be hard to find someone who understands our unique situation. But that isolation that we used to feel with family and friends has long since left us. We talk freely about our problems, and we have developed skills to help us overcome them. This has allowed us to make many friends with shared experiences. Some are families with special needs children. Some aren't.

The problems that we face are usually no different than any other family, but they can become more complex because of my son's communication challenges. Because of his condition, we can sometimes encounter unique challenges that family and friends may not understand, but we can usually find common ground when we focus on the common feelings that underlie the unique circumstances. In this way, we've learned to embrace our unique lives without falling into isolation or loneliness.

It isn't all bad. Despite my son's challenges with language and emotions, there are a number of extraordinary skills that he possesses. He has been diagnosed as a calendar savant, which he uses to dazzle family, friends, and strangers like an up-close magician on the street. At times, he has shown almost superhuman abilities with technology, puzzles, balance, memory, and even music, but each one of these skills can come as both a blessing and a curse. They can help him to make connections with the world around him, but they can also paralyze or imprison him in a confusing and isolated world. These unique abilities are a challenge

## THE GOOD, THE BAD, AND THE UGLY

at times, making it even more difficult to understand and connect with other people—including me, but they also create interesting opportunities for connections. With patience and tolerance, these skills have often served as a starting point for communication and problem-solving. As a result, our lives have proved to be a fascinating adventure.

At times, every parent feels helpless in securing their children's futures. At times, all people feel vulnerable and threatened. But problems in special needs families often loom larger and more intensely. Plans and expectations are always in peril, constantly shifting, and often unattainable. Real worries in the present or about the future compound a parent's own security issues—often made more difficult as a result of the family's special needs. Ordinary social obstacles like friendship, love, and community become more complex and challenging for both parent and child.

Our household challenges aren't unique despite my child's unique challenges. Every day, another family is confronted by a special needs diagnosis. It's unfair that a child's life will be fraught with unforeseen obstacles through no fault of their own. The feeling of powerlessness that comes from a special needs diagnosis is very real. To realize that a child will face challenges to everyday living, often with chronic health problems or even a shortened lifespan, is heartbreaking. No parent is equipped for the self-doubt, frustration, or isolation that the diagnosis inevitably brings. But there is a silver lining.

If faced honestly, fearlessly, and humbly, a special needs life carries significant rewards for everyone in the family. Free from society's pressures, special needs children often grow into beacons of love. In many instances, they are able to tap into a joy and intimacy that is out of reach for most of us in this competitive world. Like divining rods, they often pull the best qualities from their parents, friends, and the strangers they encounter. Their very lives force us to rethink measures for life, success, value, and importance. They easily overcome barriers of race, class, and gender, presenting a valuable example for society at large. They can truly be measured by their effect on those around them—beginning with their parents.

That's the purpose of this book, to help families struggling with a special needs child in emotional crisis. I am not an expert in overcoming special needs, but those experts are easy enough to find in any community. I am only an expert in my family's experience. I have learned to use that experience, and I hope that this helps others find solutions that work for them.

In the next chapter, we will explore the crisis and what is really going on inside the parent's mind, so that we can better understand it in our children and society at large. In chapter 3, we will explore the different buttons that people press and how those buttons push us toward crisis. Then, we will take a closer look at those drives that threaten all families but pose critical problems when families are coming to terms with special needs members of the family. We begin to see how it warps our perspectives and generates a whole spectrum of emotions that hurtle us toward crisis.

Chapter 4 digs into the very real security issues—financial, emotional and physical—that can overwhelm parents of special needs children. Chapter 5 addresses those significant social threats that drive families with special needs children into isolation. Chapter 6 explores how our plans, expectations, and routines—both ours and our children's—can lead to the very crisis that they are designed to avoid.

Chapter 7 targets the challenges of divorce, separation, or dysfunction that plague families with special needs children even more than the public at large. How does a broken family mend? How do parents overcome differences in parenting styles, competitions between households, and long-standing hurts in order to function as a whole?

Finally, as we develop solutions for our own problems, we begin to see how our children are facing similar difficulties. We develop ways to support them in their growth. Chapter 8 focuses on the communication issues faced by a parent when his or her child has communication issues that impact the ability to handle simple life challenges. How can a special needs child handle complex life challenges—like emotions—without the simple language skills necessary?

Once parent and child are no longer in conflict, we begin to see how we can better relate to the world around us. Over the next three chapters we look at problems that seem to loom large in homes with special needs.

Chapter 9 takes a look at puberty and other life challenges that can test even the most established coping techniques. How do we survive major life changes or the death of family and friends? How does a parent's role change as our children become adults?

Chapter 10 looks at educational challenges and how to rise to the challenge of team meetings and performance reviews. How do parents navigate these well-meaning, necessary, but often overwhelming meetings with school boards, teachers and specialists? What unique insight can we bring to these meetings, and what can we take away from them to help us in our everyday lives?

Finally, chapter 11 returns to my family's personal story and the hope that we built through the practice of these techniques. I learned that, in order to help my son through his struggles, I had to deal with mine. As a result, we developed better ways to communicate. I found ways to reach him by sharing my own experience. We developed ideals for our home life and a healthy family life after divorce. My life improved, my son's life improved, and we began to flourish as a family. Dealing with my son's condition was the most difficult obstacle I've had to overcome, but I wouldn't trade the experience for anything.

# THE GOOD, THE BAD, AND THE UGLY

Except for a few difficult moments and some challenging phases, our lives have become peaceful and purpose-driven. We have been able to help families like ours in finding their own solutions to these common problems.

Practicing this solution has also had an impact outside of our household. In this world of growing pressures, many people are often on the brink of crisis. As my son and I have become more adept at dealing with crisis in our lives, we've been able to become better members of society. Armed with this new perspective, we started to relate differently to the stressful world around us. One of my greatest joys is to see my son grow into a confident, sensitive young man. He cares about others. He has become a source of peace, comfort, and joy in my household and in the lives of those around us. I've seen him offer comfort and support that goes well beyond his language skills. He's become a useful member of society and a valuable person in our small circle.

Our lives aren't perfect. Like all people, we have good days and bad days, but over time our lives continue to improve. My son's condition has no cure, so it will continue for his lifetime. But it has opened up doors that I never could have imagined. Like most people, he will face obstacles with various degrees of failure and success, but he has developed good coping skills, a great sense of humor, and the ability to offer unconditional love. We both have.

# CHAPTER TWO

*Crisis? What Crisis?*

Every day, stories like mine are playing out in homes across the nation and throughout the world because families living with special needs children are more common than many might think. According to a 2018 study, about one in forty-four children in the United States has been identified with autism spectrum disorder.[1] A more recent study found that approximately one in six children (ages three to seventeen) were diagnosed with some kind of developmental disorder,[2] and that was a steady increase from previous studies.

According to US Census Data from 2020 there are more than 73.1 million Americans under eighteen years of age. If one in six of them have developmental disorders, that could be almost 12.5 million special needs children in the United States, alone. If the rate holds true in other countries, there could be as many as 400 million special needs children around the world at any given time.

Each one of those households is grappling with increased physical, social, and economic challenges that lead many to frustration and isolation. Sleepless nights are full of worries as parents contemplate their uncertain futures and those of their children. That leads to even more frustration and isolation. Eventually, many will find themselves in that state of crisis I described in the previous chapter. Almost every one of us can think of a neighbor, a friend, or a family member whose daily lives have been affected by disorders, but unless you've experienced it yourself there is no possibility of fully understanding the state of crisis that can permeate our waking moments. Overcoming this emotional crisis is the main focus of this book.

Every parent has bad days, but a crisis is something else entirely. At certain times, most parents wrestle with frustration, anger, and worry for their children, and sometimes that results in a parental meltdown. These bad moments take many forms. A spoiled child demands something in the checkout line at a grocery store, and the frustrated parent erupts into an embarrassing tantrum. Two siblings are fighting endlessly in the back seat, and the angry driver pulls off to the shoulder for an irrational rant. A child is caught in an emotional crisis, and the parent storms off to escape. The list goes on and on.

These breakdowns can ruin an afternoon. A single incident can destroy the family's peace for a whole day, and they rarely fix the problem. If parents lose their cool once in a while, it might even work. An angry scold could temporarily halt a child's bad behavior, but the results are always short-lived. Angry parenting rarely changes behavior for good. In fact, the more a parent dips into this nuclear arsenal, the less effective that tool becomes. It never brings the family closer together.

For most parents these moments are rare—even though they may come more often during certain stages of a child's development. What parent doesn't have horror stories about the dreaded "terrible twos" or those tumultuous "tween years?" Ask any parent with grown children what it was like to live with them during those hormonal teenage years, and that will spark a long conversation. But when a child's development is delayed, those "normal" stages of development can come later and last longer. A two-year-old's meltdown is annoying, but when it happens in the body of a five-year-old or tween, it can be physically dangerous. Normal stages of growth and independence are difficult enough, but when a child is also dealing with communication issues, physical limitations, or health complications, these life chapters become more challenging.

In those early days when a child is struggling without a diagnosis, a parent's "bad days" can begin to bleed together and steam out of control. The child lacks the necessary tools for daily living, and the parent lacks the tools to provide real help. As both struggle with this unsolvable problem, frustrations build. After a while, an emotional fatigue descends upon the household as one day's irritation bleeds into the next. Before the diagnosis comes, there's a sort of flying-blind phase where solutions are temporary at best. At the same time, medical treatments shift from wildly inconsistent to terribly ineffective. Confusion, worry, and anger become commonplace as parents force solutions to problems that they don't even understand. When parent and child erupt in daily battles, it can no longer be dismissed as a bad day. This constant state of conflict becomes the new norm—a day entrenched in crisis.

A crisis can lead to anything from an angry collision between parent and child to a desperate attempt to escape the situation. Emotional outbursts are followed by waves of guilt and feelings of inferiority in the parent as they are forced to confront their own inadequacy. On one extreme, the family home becomes a battlefield with arguments breaking out everywhere. On the other extreme, everybody withdraws to their own camps, the home falls into disarray, and the family begins to struggle with basic functions like hygiene and health care. Both extremes can cause a wide range of damage, from hurt feelings to court dates. Worse, these moments can become an ordinary fact of life, so that our meltdowns and tantrums—and those of our child—seem almost normal.

Recently, I came across a friend of mine with a special needs child, and she was engaged in a conversation with a friend over coffee. Her son sat nearby, rocking uncomfortably and muttering to himself. It was good to see them in public, but it was clear that my friend's attention was divided between her guest across the table and her child's growing unease. The situation accelerated quickly. The boy broke out into repetitive speech and began moaning. People at nearby tables kept glancing over at him as his behavior continued to unravel. Then, in an instant, my friend tensed up and spun around toward her son.

"Shut up. Shut up! SHUT UP!" she yelled. Then, just as quickly, she returned to her conversation as the echo shook the room.

Her coffee companion looked stunned. People at nearby tables looked shocked. I stopped dead in my tracks. But my friend, totally unaware of her outburst, returned to her conversation as if nothing had happened.

Now, this might have seemed strange to everyone else in the coffee shop, but in special needs homes this sort of behavior can be more common than we'd like to admit. Sure, there might be a little more self-awareness during or after our meltdowns, but a parent in crisis can probably recall dozens of examples where a reaction might have been just as sudden, irrational, and inappropriate as my friend's reaction to her fidgeting child. The child did nothing to justify the explosive reaction. By any measure, my friend's response was incredibly selfish and unloving, but I can certainly sympathize with the state of mind that would draw such a backlash from a normally loving and selfless person.

If stressed-out parents are being truly honest with themselves, these sorts of reactions—even if they are only in our heads—are more common than we'd like to admit. Early in my son's development, these moments of crisis were practically a daily occurrence.

There also seems to be little chance of avoiding these moments of crisis no matter how hard a parent tries, and that's strange considering the strength and discipline that it takes to be a parent in a special needs home. Forgetting a favorite toy can be devastating to an errand, so we choreograph complex preparations for even the shortest trip from the home. Forgetting an important item on a grocery list would require a return to the store, so we develop disciplined approaches to these simple tasks. Balancing work duties, parenting responsibilities, and daily schedules takes an enormous amount of planning and discipline, yet these very strengths seem to quickly vanish in an instant during those moments of crisis.

There are three ways that this state of crisis builds in a parent. The most common comes from enduring long periods of stress. Fatigue creeps into our lives through a series of events. The parent doesn't see the pattern of difficulties until it's too late. All the pent-up stress pours out in an uncontrollable moment of crisis. Afterward, it's easy to see how the pattern developed, but in the moment there are few signs that a crisis is coming. Here's a good illustration:

Imagine that you're behind the wheel of a brand-new car, winding your way along a river to meet some friends at the beach. The sun is shining. The car handles perfectly, and there's nobody else on the road. The radio plays a medley of your favorite songs as you come to a red light. You'd likely just stop and wait for the light to turn green. Right? You might fall into a daydream or take in the scenery, but there would be no crisis over a single red light. There would be no frustration or loss of your peaceful state.

But as clouds begin to gather on the horizon or a string of red lights begins to throw off your schedule, would your reaction change with each additional nuisance? As each delay becomes more of a problem, frustration piles up. When would it be the breaking point? Would it take ten lights? One hundred?

There are a lot of other factors that could affect that breaking point. What if, instead of a day with friends, we were racing to an important job interview? What if we were running late? What if we were focused on a financial problem or an argument with a family member? What if the radio station kept cutting out? What if we had just received an emergency phone call and were racing to the hospital? As problems pile up, that next traffic light—or even the first one—might prove the tipping point.

The tipping point, of course, is that moment when the driver has lost all perspective. It's that moment of crisis when an ordinarily good driver turns to road rage, or the overwhelmed parent begins to melt down. For a parent with a special needs child, this illustration fits perfectly. The red lights are the perfect metaphor for my son's tantrums in those early days, or the obstacles posed at each turn in our daily journey. We became locked in a one-way competition with everybody and everything around us in a way that made it impossible for anybody to win.

Of course, there are other obstacles that might add to our frustration—commuter traffic, road construction, bad weather, or an irate driver hanging on our back bumper. How I pity that poor, unsuspecting driver who pulls out in front of us, or that overly cautious driver in front of us who stops for a yellow light. It might be their first intersection of the day, but for us it's the final straw.

In fact, there is no real difference between the situation at the first red light or the hundredth. The only difference is the state of mind of the driver. For an emotional driver, the red light poses a threat. As problems pile up in the car, on the road, or in the life of the driver, the driver begins to focus more on the obstacles and less on the needs of anyone else on the road—even their passenger. At some point, drivers can become so strained that it affects their judgment. Drivers can fall so out of balance that they actually blame the light for turning red or disregard it entirely. Many people spend their whole lives blaming red lights.

For a parent of a special needs child in crisis, the daily commute doesn't start with a bright blue sky or the perfect soundtrack. Yesterday's trip, today's traffic, and tomorrow's breakdown are already weighing on the mind of the driver long before we turn the key, and it grows heavier with each red light we encounter. Feelings of worry, frustration, and isolation continue to mount. Simple routines become more tedious and complex. A mundane task like a trip to the grocery store gets mired in dozens of detours and work-arounds. One trip leads into the next until it can be overwhelming to just turn the key. Even when a task does go off without a hitch, it is often filled with moments of fear and anxiety.

As obstacles mount, they tear at the fabric of the family. Those intimate motivations prized in a parent—love and unselfishness—slowly get replaced by competition as parents try to get situations to work out in their favor. The child and parent find themselves locked in a competition, and that competition leads to crisis.

When he was young, my son's language issues manifested in frequent temper tantrums. They would come out of nowhere and rage endlessly. They seemed to come at the most inopportune times, and I spent much of my day trying to avoid or control those outbursts. I came to dread his meltdowns, and I would develop elaborate plans to avoid or minimize them. As soon as I'd enter a family gathering, I'd begin to script my escape. I'd over-explain my son's state of mind, and heap advice for avoiding meltdowns on everyone as if I was the director on a movie set. Store visits would include carry-on bags filled with distractions. Late entrances, quiet conversations, and interactions were choreographed with precision. Even simple tasks became challenges, and his behavior seemed to influence every decision we made throughout the day. Attending a crowded birthday party tortured him ... and, eventually, me. Drop-in visits or sudden changes to our schedule created problems for him ... and for me. Unforeseen problems baffled both of us.

Because of the cost of one-on-one supervision, childcare wasn't an option for us. As a single parent, there weren't many opportunities to escape for a quick errand like a simple oil change. My son and I often had to travel together if we were to accomplish those menial daily tasks that everybody needs to complete. It was impossible to prepare for every contingency, so the threat of a meltdown lay around every corner and at every delay. Trying to navigate that challenge is the main problem for the parent of a special needs child. Any wrong turn, any mistake can seem daunting. Still, I rarely saw the pattern of stresses build as I fought for control ... until it reached the breaking point.

Of course, it wasn't always such a straight line to a crisis. Often, the tipping point was less predictable than a simple string of stoplights. There are times when, looking back on a meltdown, it's hard to understand why it even started. The event that sparks the meltdown, in retrospect, seems trivial. I believe that this is what happened to my friend in the coffee shop.

Why is it that an old, persistent behavior returns after a long period of absence, or a parent crumbles at the first instance?

Why, after mastering a persistent problem with patience and tolerance, does a parent suddenly struggle at the start of the next problem? Why don't the well-practiced survival mechanisms work when the behavior returns after a long absence or a new one emerges? This is the second way a crisis manifests, and patterns leading up to it are harder to recognize.

A parent's reaction during this sort of crisis is baffling, and the response is usually much worse than the behavior that sparked it. Even when a parent has displayed incredible patience throughout the day or has shown remarkable patience just a few moments earlier, the meltdown is unexpected and chaotic. With this sort of crisis, there is still a pattern, but we have to take a much wider view in order to see it emerge. This crisis doesn't build through a pattern of repeating issues, it emerges from a string of seemingly unrelated obstacles. This is actually one of the most common ways that a crisis emerges. Seemingly unrelated issues with planning, security and society overlap, complicate each other, and hurtle an unsuspecting person toward crisis. It's difficult to see a crisis of this sort building.

My friend Reno likes to share an example of this sort of crisis that has nothing to do with a special needs child, but special needs parents can certainly relate to it. His episode happened during a typical workday that led up to a scheduled dentist appointment. Throughout his day, he handled various challenges with grace and dignity until one seemingly unrelated obstacle proved to be the tipping point.

I meet Reno regularly for a morning coffee with a group of our friends. We get together often before heading off to work. On this particular day, we all arrived late, and the coffee wasn't ready. Everyone seemed to get sidetracked into different conversations, and Reno was forced to leave for work before the coffee was served. Despite the delays and disruptions, he was able to bow out gracefully without his morning brew.

In fact, he seemed to handle obstacles with ease throughout his day. He got caught in traffic on his way to work, but he was able to relax and let it go. There was no road rage, no mounting stress. He realized that the time he arrived at work was out of his immediate control. When he finally clocked in, nobody seemed too troubled.

He is employed in a very busy kitchen, so a typical day has a hectic pace with a flurry of deadlines and obstacles. On this particular day, he took everything in stride. His boss kept shifting demands, but he was able to juggle every ball thrown his way. On the other hand, it took longer than usual to finish, so he had to hurry to his dentist appointment at the end of the day. He arrived about five minutes late, leaped from his car, and raced toward the office. He burst through the door to find a patient receptionist who didn't seem too worried about his tardiness.

As Reno took his seat in the waiting room, *the receptionist pointed out a small problem with his insurance …*

## PARENT IN CRISIS

My friend had shown patience throughout his day. He overcame every hurdle in his path and seemed unshakable with every delay—at our morning meeting, during the delay in traffic, and with the shifting demands at work—until that poor receptionist delivered the news about his insurance. That small obstacle was the final straw. My friend unleashed the whole day's frustration on that poor, unsuspecting receptionist, and every stress he had overcome throughout the day came pouring out. He returned the next day to apologize, but he spent the next couple of weeks looking for a new dentist.

It may be more difficult to see the pattern emerge with these sorts of meltdowns, but there is one. Reno was facing stoplights all day. There were disruptions to his plans and expectations. There were money issues, and there were social hurdles. Even though he was putting out fires all day, the heat was building. Subtly, subconsciously, his emotional issues piled up.

This was certainly a bad day for my friend, but as parents of special needs children, we face these sorts of challenges every day. It might seem out of character when a parent who balances child meltdowns, workday issues, hectic schedules, doctor's visits, and delays with ease suddenly unravels in an instant when presented with a small, unrelated problem that pales in light of everything else. But to a parent of a special needs child, this makes perfect sense.

On the other hand, a state of crisis doesn't always build

logically. Sometimes, a crisis seems to erupt out of nowhere. This is the hardest type to avoid or predict. A day might be working out perfectly. Everything might be going smoothly with no previous problems and no outside stressors. There might not be a single red light in our day's journey. Then, with no warning, one appears. With our defenses down, the very first obstacle thrusts us into crisis.

One of my best examples of this was a meltdown in a parking lot when my son was just a toddler. One weekend, my friend Bob had invited my son and me to breakfast. We had spent a peaceful morning at a local diner, but after the uneventful meal, we bumped into one of Bob's friends in the parking lot who was going through some difficulties in his life. The three of us talked for almost half an hour until my son began to squirm in my arms.

Excusing myself from the conversation, *I returned to my car just in time for my son's tantrum ...*

We battled with his car seat like professional wrestlers in the ring. He scratched at my face as I wrangled with the restraints. I could feel a bead of blood on my chin as I clicked the clasp on his seat belt. I stepped back to slam the door ... and stepped right onto Bob's foot. He was watching our car seat battle, but I hadn't been aware of the audience.

I did what I was programmed to do whenever I noticed somebody was watching us. I whirled around, wiped the blood off my chin, and twisted my face into a crooked smile. "I didn't see you there," I said sweetly.

He wasn't fooled. "You should be ashamed of yourself."

"Why should *I* be ashamed?"

He just shook his head. "You just finished talking to a complete stranger, and you were nothing but loving and tolerant. Then, you treated your son—the person you love most in the world—like this? You should be ashamed of yourself."

His words stung, but I had to admit that he was right. I felt good about the way I carried myself during the talk with his friend. I had been patient, self-sacrificing, and honest as we discussed the man's problem in the parking lot. Then, just a few moments later, I was impatient, selfish, and demanding with my son as we got into our car. I didn't even see it coming, and my actions made perfect sense to me as we wrestled with the car seat. I had lost all perspective with the first obstacle I faced that day, and I reacted poorly.

All three types of crisis share some common symptoms. Parents lose perspective in an emotional moment, and they lose control of themselves. The selfish and unloving behavior that spills out completely opposes their normal parenting. The ensuing tantrum leaves feelings of embarrassment, guilt, and remorse in its wake—along with the firm resolution that we will act better the next time. But in the moment of crisis, there's no realization that we are acting poorly at all. In fact, our reactions seem justified and normal. Sometimes a parent might even deny that they acted poorly at all.

Sure, a parent's reactions might be more harsh or more subtle than these examples, but behaviors are never good when a parent is in crisis. At best, it's an emotional game of Russian roulette. The tipping point is different for everybody, and most people won't see it coming. Almost every irrational parenting decision can be traced back to this emotional state.

Most parents will be unable to see the growing crisis until it's too late, but parents of special needs children do not have this luxury given the impact our outbreaks have on our children. Unless we are aware of our emotional state before we reach the tipping point, we will be unable to avoid those irrational outbursts that follow. We must develop self-awareness long before there's a problem in front of us, or we are doomed.

This is not a simple task, but we must learn to spot those impending blank spots. One good way is to reflect on the past day—good or bad. At some point during the day, it is helpful to go back over the events and ask ourselves three simple questions.

The first question is, "When was I closest to that moment of crisis?" It should be easy enough to spot for parents who are wrestling with the stressors of a special needs household. We are looking for those emotional moments where we were approaching that irrational tipping point. If we look hard enough, there will be very few days when we can't find something that fits this definition. Even if we didn't erupt in a tantrum, we can identify those moments when we were closest to the breaking point. We might have been nursing a grudge, or we might have been annoyed or frustrated. Often, the emotional blank spot is seen as a subtle moment of panic when we forget something important. It might be a time when we were too tired to get involved while our child was acting up. Rarely is there a day when no moment can be found.

Once we've identified the moment when we were closest to crisis, we should ask if we were honest about our state of mind? Did we realize we were approaching a moment of crisis? For most of us, we'll find that we were totally unaware that we were approaching any tipping point. There was no reason to guard against a meltdown because we were under the delusion that everything was under control.

Finally, we can look at our actions in this irrational state of mind and question our behavior. Were we thinking about our child's struggles or our own? How was our patience? When the situation was not to our liking, were we getting upset? Were we digging in our heels over something unimportant? Were we trying to force solutions? Were we trying to get our way? Did we withhold love? Did we have controlling, twisted motives—even good ones?

If we are being honest with ourselves, we will have to admit that we are usually unaware of the building crisis. Even worse, there is usually very little conscious thought about the actions that follow that tipping point. We may work very hard to be self-sacrificing, patient, tolerant, and loving throughout the day, but in those moments of crisis we find that there's little thought to anyone's needs but our own. It happens without any realization on our part.

If we are disciplined in our daily review, it will pay dividends right away. First, we will be able to see that most of us do much better than we think. Although these moments of crisis may occur more often than we'd like, we will usually find plenty of moments that should have brought crisis but didn't. In fact, most of us will identify many moments when unbelievable patience came almost automatically. By comparing those moments with our moments of crisis, we will gain a better perspective on our own state of mind. We will begin to see the long string of lights that we handled intuitively and will be able to compare them with the one red light that troubled us.

As we continue our daily review, those moments of crisis become a sort of measuring stick for us. We will be able to see trends—good and bad. We will be able to set goals for future behavior and measure our progress. Most importantly, we will find that this self-awareness becomes a valuable tool. As we get better at identifying our successes and failures at the end of the day, we become better at seeing them in the present, and ultimately, we become able to recognize them before they happen. We can begin to see that tipping point looming when there's still time to avoid it. For a parent of a special needs child who often feels overwhelmed and confused, this is the golden ticket.

There's another advantage to this practice. As we develop an awareness of these moments of crisis within us, we begin to see them developing in our children. It didn't take long before I began to see how much I had in common with my son. As I became adept at spotting my own blank spots, I began to see how these moments of crisis grew in him. That helped me understand his bad behavior better than I ever could have before. I began to see how his anger and rage grew from other, unresolved emotions. Without language, he lacked the tools to identify these emotions, let alone try to solve them. If unchecked, his anxieties led to rage. If he was confused, sad, worried, or anxious—and it wasn't addressed—it would turn to anger. Even good emotions, like excitement—even joy—would often transform into rage if he didn't understand the feelings.

As I saw his struggles with his emotions, I began to add those emotions to my own daily inventory. In a very concrete way, I was able to see how I handled those same feelings or—just as importantly—where I fell short. By learning about myself, I gained more empathy for my son's struggles. Armed with this perspective, I was able to describe his emotions on his behalf and help him develop strategies to deal with them. I could show him what worked for me and what didn't. Then, I could help him practice these solutions independently.

Identifying the crisis was just the beginning, but it was a good starting point for everything that followed. As I focused on those moments of crisis that I had missed throughout my day, I became more disciplined at spotting them in the moment.

Sometimes, I was even able to see them as they were building. With greater self-awareness, I found that, even during his moments of crisis, I was improving my ability to offer my son the patience, tolerance, and love that he deserved because I was consciously aware of my emotional state and better able to envision my options. In that state of self-awareness, it becomes more difficult to justify bad behavior and easier to recognize emotions building in others—even my son. Coping mechanisms could be implemented before my meltdown and better modeled before my son's crisis exploded. Slowly, those moments of crisis—his and mine—became less common. Even when they did manifest, they weren't as troubling or long-lasting. I could finally see the light at the end of the tunnel because I was armed with a better understanding of the problem and more practiced with solutions that worked.

There was another, unintended benefit that I received from this daily review. As I developed more self-awareness for both myself and my son, I developed a better understanding of other people. I was no longer as consumed with my own problems, and I began to see that others struggled, too. Although their problems were different than mine, I began to see those same emotions that troubled me as they began to build in family, friends, and strangers that I encountered throughout the day. Seen in this light, it became easier to begin treating others with the same compassion and understanding that I was trying to develop with myself and my child.

Not that I treated people poorly before this, but as I became more adept at seeing other people from their perspectives, it marked another turning point in my life. I began to see how addressing my son's special needs helped me to solve my own problems, and I became more useful to others around me.

Of course, we must go further than just identifying the moments of crisis in our lives. We have to be able to identify the underlying causes if we are going to be of real help to ourselves, our children, and those around us. In the next chapter, we will get down to causes and conditions. What brings about these moments of crisis? Can we learn to avoid them entirely? Can we learn to find peace and a sense of purpose during these moments of crisis? Can we get to the point where we no longer need to avoid anger, fear, anxiety or worry?

The answer to all of these questions is "yes," but first we'll need to get down to causes and conditions. We will need to know what sparks those moments of crisis if we are to have any hope of avoiding them.

[1] Maenner MJ, Shaw KA, Bakian AV, et al; Prevalence and Characteristics of Autism Spectrum Disorder Among Children Aged 8 Years; Autism and Developmental Disabilities Monitoring Network, 2018.
[2] Cogswell ME et al; Health Needs and Use of Services Among Children with Developmental Disabilities; Morbidity and Mortality Weekly Report, 2022.

# CHAPTER THREE

*The Balancing Act: Underlying Issues*

---

Before drifting off to sleep, I like to review the hours that passed. I rarely encounter a day that hasn't included some sort of emotional crisis. When times are stressful, they are easy to recognize, but we can just as easily fall into emotional turmoil when things are going well for us. That's the most bewildering issue about a parent in crisis. Sometimes, the flash point comes out of nowhere. At other times, emotions build progressively toward a boiling point. Even when our day is going smoothly, it seems that there's always some sort of potential crisis hiding just around the corner. No matter how much we try, parents of special needs children will often find it impossible to avoid a meltdown entirely. Sometimes, it feels as if our lives are spent hopping from one crisis to another.

At first, it may surprise us how often we are in emotional

turmoil throughout the day, especially during that tumultuous journey toward a diagnosis. Often, our lives feel like a sadistic game of emotional "whack-a-mole." We can throw ourselves into solving a serious financial problem, only to have some sort of social crisis pop up. When that issue is resolved, a health problem pops up. Doctors' visits, work issues, competing schedules, and future worries seem to erupt all around us. A state of crisis is always within reach when we are juggling so many outside threats.

When stressed-out parents succumb to their emotions—which they commonly do—the ensuing behavior is often wildly erratic. Engulfed by crisis, a typically honest and straightforward parent might suddenly transform into a twisted and calculating puppet master. Facing an enormous threat, a normally patient and loving person might transmute into an overly demanding monster. During an emotional spree, traits like humility, generosity, and patience are quickly cast aside for some sort of negative reaction. Parents in crisis get locked into a self-defense mode, retaliating against anyone and everything in their path like giant wrecking balls. Most often, the targets for our meltdowns are those people closest to us. Too often, it's our special needs child themselves. A parent in crisis often alternates between these Jekyll and Hyde extremes.

Special needs parents often find themselves struggling to balance emotions and relationships in and out of the family. We can become deluged by self-pity, depression, and frustration. We struggle to make ends meet and to build savings, so we often feel like we are falling short as parents. We feel isolated from society, useless to our community, and without a meaningful purpose in our lives. We begin to find ourselves in conflict with everybody—even ourselves. We are filled with jealousy of others, resentful for our plight, and overwhelmed with fear about the challenges our children will face. We feel misunderstood by those closest to us. We are filled with concern about our future and about our children's future after we die. We feel selfish when we worry about our own needs, and we feel guilt and remorse when we prioritize our own needs over our children. We are constantly second-guessing our life choices, and we are overwhelmed by every small decision. In that state, it is impossible to find even one moment of peace.

Eventually, a special needs parent can lose so much perspective that we won't even be able to admit that we are suffering. Ask how we are doing, and we might mutter, "Fine," even when it's clear to everyone else that we are spinning out of control. If you strapped us to a lie detector test in that instant, we'd probably pass with flying colors. The ability to think clearly and act rationally evaporates during an emotional crisis. Once the monster is unleashed, we find ourselves fighting through turmoil like angry children trying to get their way at all costs.

In fact, until an emotional spree loses its steam, there is usually little chance of controlling our behavior. The tantrum will have to exhaust itself before an angry parent is able to resume a loving position in the family. Relief from an internal struggle must come before a detached parent can reengage. This is the real catastrophe for a parent in crisis and the real reason why a daily inventory is such an important first step. It is a good practice to identify those moments of crisis at the end of each day, but it would be even better to find a way to avoid the damaging emotional spree altogether. That means that we will have to find a way to be proactive because it isn't enough to just spot the tipping point. We must learn to identify those underlying problems before they build into a crisis. This practice takes time and effort that only a parent in crisis would be willing to invest.

So what is it that drives us toward a crisis? It is easy to see that, when we feel hurt or threatened, we react poorly. In fact, many of our meltdowns can be seen as a reaction to other people, including our children. We defend ourselves and our children against any unfairness of circumstances, and we desperately try to regain control of any negativity directed toward us. But this is only half the story.

If we are being honest with ourselves, we can admit that we are often able to act well when things aren't going our way, or people aren't acting properly. Parents of special needs children can usually cite examples by the dozen where we have maintained our composure in situations that would have flustered most reasonable people. But when we are in crisis, our actions are anything but composed. Why does a parent overreact that one time after successfully handling a similar situation dozens of times? Finding

## THE BALANCING ACT

the answer to that question is much more important than pointing fingers at the person or situation that sparked our rage.

Most of us find that emotional meltdowns come most frequently when our guard is down, so the tipping point in most of those situations typically comes when we least expect it. We may have endured a particular problem all day, but we overreact as soon as the pressure lets up. Even though we have the discipline to react well most of the time, meltdowns happen most frequently in the home when we're fatigued, hungry, or emotional. How many times have work issues spilled out at the dinner table or the bus stop? Often it's those closest to us, those we love the most and need us the most, who encounter our worst behaviors. Many times it's our special needs children themselves.

Of course every person is different, so every parent is different. The actual tipping point for any crisis will vary from person to person. In fact, it can change from day to day or even shift throughout the day, but those moments of crisis always seem to erupt at times when our guard is down and we feel out of balance. Since it is impossible to keep our guard up indefinitely (so many of us have tried and failed at this), then finding balance is crucial. Everybody feels unbalanced at times, but it's especially true in a household that's struggling to live with special needs. We are constantly being pushed and pulled in different directions, and we always seem headed for crisis. It's a little like trying to balance a three-armed scale.

To achieve balance, it is necessary to understand what we are trying to balance in the first place. That daily review gives us important insight. After learning to identify those moments of crisis, we can begin to look deeper at the underlying causes and conditions to better understand how the crisis develops. The first thing we notice is that every crisis checks at least one of three boxes. Crisis usually erupts when our security is threatened, when a social problem can't be solved, or when we encounter an obstacle to our plans and routines. The intensity of our reaction usually depends on how many threats are perceived at once, the severity of any one of those threats, and the persistence of a vulnerable state. Although each of these issues is explored in depth over the next three chapters, we can look at them more generally now:

Security issues abound in special needs homes. So many moments of crisis flare up from problems in this area. There are so many outside threats to our daily living that security issues often go unnoticed until one finally proves too much. It doesn't seem to matter if an issue is physical, emotional, mental, or financial. Overlapping security problems continue to pile up until a parent becomes overwhelmed. There were many times when my son was in turmoil, and I spent much of my day fighting off his attacks or tending to his meltdowns. Trapped in that constant state of physical insecurity, encountering a small financial problem might prove too much. Especially when we were first coming to grips with my son's disabilities, it felt like I was riding an emotional roller coaster. There were so many threats to our daily lives that it was inevitable that one would eventually spark crisis. When living in such a severe state of insecurity, anything can pose a serious dilemma.

By developing more self-awareness, it becomes easier to proactively address growing insecurities before they become overwhelming. As I became more disciplined at recognizing insecurity issues, I began to develop better coping mechanisms. I realized that, after a physical altercation with my son, I needed to address my feelings of insecurity. It is amazing how a few deep breaths before continuing, allowing myself a moment to regroup, or forcing a slower pace could mean the difference between a calm and successful trip or a moment of crisis. When a cool head prevails, we can make much better decisions—even when insecurities seem to be piling up.

Relationship issues and social threats permeate the lives of special needs families, but these conditions are often more subtle and difficult to identify. Communication issues, self-esteem issues, feelings of chronic loneliness, and power dynamics seem to pummel us on certain days. We struggle with red tape, bureaucracy, and relationships. We run into problems getting along with everyone, especially those in authority. As a result, living in a special needs home can be very isolating. Parents, like their children, can feel like they are outsiders in every situation they encounter. It is no wonder that social problems can build into a crisis. Any time we feel that society has wronged us or that people are treating us unfairly, we can get locked in a "fight-or-flight" response. Often, we don't see the crisis coming until it's too late to stop it.

It is interesting to note that social threats don't have to be directed at us to spark a response. Take a common problem like getting cut off in traffic. Whether it's fear or anger, our reaction will certainly depend on how much our safety and security are threatened, but our reaction will be more intense if our child is in the passenger's seat. That's because a perceived threat or injury to a family member or friend has more potential to spark a crisis in us than a direct threat or injury to ourselves.

When someone else is involved, it almost always complicates the emotional response. A security problem that affects someone close to us is both a security problem and a social issue. Since two problems usually seem bigger than one, a problem that affects both us and our child is more likely to spark a crisis in us. Even if we're unaffected, threats or injuries to our children frequently spark a strong reflex. A big enough threat perceived against our special needs children can spark an instantaneous response. It's also easier to justify bad behavior when we are protecting or defending someone else. By learning to identify those mounting social strains on us and those closest to us, we can address them with some measure of grace and dignity if we can catch ourselves before we reach crisis.

Ambitions were also a common culprit when it came to

moments of crisis. When my son's problems began to manifest, it threatened every plan and expectation that I had for my life and his. Uncertainty, fear, and anxiety were everyday companions, and our days soon became overscheduled. Our routines were demanding, rigid, and dependent on so many factors that were outside of our control. Should it surprise anyone that obstacles to my plans or his created crisis? Frequently, it felt as if everyone and everything was working against us. At times, it still feels like that. When somebody or something unexpected threatens my plans, spoils my expectations, or upsets my schedule, it can easily spark a crisis.

Nobody likes to feel vulnerable or hurt, but in a special needs home that vulnerability takes on a life of its own. Issues with security, relationships, and aspirations trouble everyone, but no group is more vulnerable than people with special needs. Whether those special needs are physical, emotional or mental, a child with special needs will always be vulnerable in ways that others cannot even imagine. Parents cannot shake worries that our special needs children will face lifelong struggles with education, careers, relationships, financial security, and social standing. Even worse is the realization that we won't always be there to protect them. Under the chronic weight of these worries, encountering a simple security issue, a small social problem, or one failed plan might tip the emotional scales into crisis.

Fears about our special needs children complicate every decision that we make, so parents often find themselves in a cruel tug of war between our short-term objectives and their long-term ramifications. By sacrificing careers to attend to our children, we worry about the impact it will have on them down the road. If we go the other way and devote ourselves to our careers and savings, it can strain our relationships with our family and friends. Financial success will almost certainly jeopardize the child's eligibility for necessary services and programs. To counter these problems, we develop complex financial and legal plans, only to find ourselves in conflict with anyone who stands in the way of our plans.

In a cruel twist of fate, every time we devote effort toward one area, it seems to make us more vulnerable somewhere else. If we throw too much effort into solving our financial problems, it can lead to strain on our relationships. If we overly focus on our child's social development, it complicates our jobs, our schedules, and our social lives. If we become too demanding about our plans, we risk driving away family and friends. Every time we devote too many resources toward reaching one goal, it seems to cause problems with others. Security, social standing, and success are impossible to achieve without creating some sort of conflict in our homes. Even in those rare moments where we do find balance, it's often shaky at best.

As a result, we find ourselves imposing so many impossible demands on ourselves, our family, and everybody else, that any plan is bound to fail. In this state of imbalance, those moments of crisis shouldn't surprise us. When we are hurt or threatened, we react in self-defense. If we are threatened deeply enough, reflex takes over. It is no surprise that this constant threatened state distorts our thinking over time. During those moments of crisis, our reactions to an outside threat can push us toward all sorts of bad behavior that we later regret. How can anyone find balance when they are weighed down by so many real and unsolvable problems?

Take, for instance, the incident that stemmed from my son's meltdown at the baseball tournament and how it sparked a crisis in me. From the moment he began to stir on the sidelines, it hurtled us into a perfect storm of instincts.

Right from the start, I had overly ambitious plans and expectations. I carefully timed my arrival with his nap schedule, so that I could take photographs of the event. My expectations were demanding and inflexible. I had good intentions because I was trying to balance my work duties with my parenting responsibilities, but I had set such high expectations for myself, a special needs toddler in a stroller, and a weekend baseball tournament run by volunteers, that my plans were unrealistic. Right from the start, my schedule was upset. I arrived too early, and the games didn't start on time. My son woke up early, and I hadn't taken as many pictures as I had hoped. At my son's first sign of unrest, I was already losing perspective.

It didn't help that I had a ton of social worries—real and imagined—that were swirling around my head. Throughout the whole event, I was worried about what everyone was thinking about me and my son, from coaches, fans, and players, to my employer (who wasn't even there). At times, it felt like they were watching the whole thing play out and judging me as a bad parent. What were people thinking about this reporter whirling around a misbehaving child and a camera? When we returned home, I was just as worried about my unseen neighbors as I was about anybody at the tournament.

Underlying everything were two big security issues related to my job and my parenting. Could I lose my job over my lack of professionalism or commitment? At the time, I was in the process of a divorce with child custody issues, so how would this all appear in court? As soon as my son began to fuss on the sidelines, I escaped in panic. Then, at home, when his tantrum turned physical, it added a safety issue on top of my other two concerns. This was when my focus shifted from his crisis to mine.

If we are unaware of building tensions, they are bound to explode. On this day—like most days—I was juggling so many plans and expectations, insecurities, and social concerns that almost anything could have set me off. Long before my son's first scream, I was already on the brink of crisis. If we are honest about most moments of crisis, we are bound to admit that being out of balance has little to do with other people. Sure, others might spark the explosion, but we are the ones packing the gunpowder. Who knows? In this particular example, my own anxiety and stress might have been the tipping point in my son's meltdown. At the very least, my state of mind proved to be a big factor as the episode unfolded.

Sometimes the threats are concrete, but others are not so easy to see. Sometimes, they aren't even real. During the baseball tournament, there was no real threat to my job. My employer was very flexible about my need to balance parenting with a weekend assignment, and it wasn't a big deal at all at the tournament. This wasn't a presidential press conference. The stands were filled with parents of young children. Nobody showed any concern about me bringing my child to work, except me, but threats don't have to make sense to be real. Whether our vulnerability is rational or irrational doesn't seem to matter in that moment of crisis. As our feelings grow in intensity, logic becomes less important.

Those intense feelings can persist whether a child's special need is mental, emotional, or physical. Crisis builds in similar ways in every special needs home. My friend's teenage daughter suffered a tragic car accident that left her with severe physical impairments. After the accident, she was confined to a wheelchair and had to face the prospect of a life with many physical and emotional challenges. She had no mental deficiencies like my son, but my son had no physical deficiencies like my friend's daughter. Despite the differences in our children's special needs, we found that our emotional situations were very similar. In both cases, the child—and the parent—were dealing with this "special need" on a daily basis, and it was affecting our security, our plans and expectations, and our relationships.

Despite our children's different special needs, my friend and I frequently talk about our common problems. We both worry that our children won't be able to earn a living, won't find a purpose or usefulness in life, and won't find an important place in the community. We are both concerned about our children's ability to build personal relationships and find romance now and in the future. We worry that our children won't be able to develop the skills needed to overcome their special needs. Will they be able to find answers for life's everyday challenges, fears, and sorrows? To be fair, these are the worries that most parents face for their children, but when that child has special needs—emotional, mental or physical—these fears are easier to justify and to act upon. Many times, the risks are very real. With my friend and me, these fears often manifested in meltdowns and crises. In fact, it seemed to affect us even more than it affected our children.

If we are going to rise above our moments of crisis, we will have to change our perspective on security issues, social stresses, and unreasonable expectations. So, how do we get there? The first step is to recognize the way we react in a crisis. When emotional, my son reacts almost subconsciously—out of reflex. To survive these meltdowns, I shift into a sort of "self-defense mode." I feel forced into making quick decisions to deal with the rising crisis, and my subconscious takes over like a cornered cat. Any outsider can see how this war of reflexes is doomed for failure. If I'm going to

# THE BALANCING ACT

be able to find peace, I have to get out of that survival mode that can rage out of control in a special needs household. To do that, I will have to make better decisions leading up to the tipping point because once the crisis begins, it's too late for self-restraint.

As emotions build toward crisis, feelings warp a parent's perspective. As we approach a meltdown, our motives begin to twist in order to avoid the problem. We begin to coach, instruct, and hover over our children. We make unreasonable demands toward others. We teach lessons. We force solutions to problems that don't even exist. Often with good motives, we create confusion and conflict with anyone in our path. When others ask about our emotions, we deny them. When they call us on our behavior, we justify it. At other times, we use brutal honesty as a weapon, calling out other people's mistakes in a twisted effort to make them comply with our demands.

Parents in crisis will find themselves in conflict with everyone and everything around them. Under normal situations a parent might be honest, self-sacrificing, and caring, but when that same parent is in crisis ... beware! Suddenly, out of nowhere, a normally fine parent becomes manipulative, self-centered, and unloving. In crisis, we often shift into a self-defense mode that makes it impossible to see any situation from any vantage point other than our own. We force our plans, forgetting that other people may have plans, too. We fight for our security even if it threatens those around us. We consider our needs, our children's needs, and those closest to us, but everyone else is treated like an obstacle. Sometimes, even our children and close family members are seen as an obstacle. The parent in crisis often reacts childishly and irrationally, blaming everyone around them for their troubles because they are so focused on themselves. During a parent's meltdown, it is impossible to see anyone else's perspective, and bad behaviors are easy to justify. Everything becomes a competition over security, relationships, and objectives, and afterward the guilt can be just as overwhelming.

We aren't different than anyone else. In today's world of fast decisions and overscheduling, most people are dealing with these same emotional challenges on a daily basis. Parents of special needs children are no different than any other parent or any other person in the world. Our challenges might seem more complex or pervasive, but they fall into the same categories as everyone else's problems. Every person confronts threats to their security, their routines, and their relationships, but many are able to find peace and purpose despite their challenges. Why, then, can't we do the same? If we are going to successfully avoid crisis, we are going to have to become aware of security issues, spoiled expectations, and social pressures before they warp our perspective too much. Then, we are going to have to change our approach to these problems.

We look to examples set by others who, like us, face daily adverse environments, yet, unlike us, handle overwhelming objectives with poise and dignity. A certain type of doctor or nurse will travel anywhere in the world to provide necessary health services. Often at great personal sacrifice to their safety and finances, they offer medical support in war-ravaged or poverty-stricken areas, far away from their family and friends. They endure hardships and danger at makeshift, underfunded hospitals. They encounter life-threatening famine, disease, and injuries. They face external pressure from bureaucracies, governments, and guerrilla groups. Why do they do it? For the peaceful and purpose-driven existence that is only available at great sacrifice to themselves.

Many religious people, driven by a selfless purpose, undertake similar missions. Like the traveling doctors, they often sacrifice their own security to travel far away from family and friends on missions of mercy and faith. They can face personal ridicule, strong opposition, and limited success, yet these missionaries often cite great benefits to this way of life as they find peace and purpose in simplicity, love, and selflessness.

There are many more examples that don't require upending our lives or traveling to distant and exotic lands. We can find examples all around us of people enduring hardship, struggles, and uncertainty to find a peaceful and purposeful existence. There are many teachers who forsake comfortable jobs in well-funded school systems to promote education in neighborhoods plagued by crime or poverty, or paraprofessionals who place themselves in harm's way, for very little pay, at a school for special needs children. Many volunteers and social workers sacrifice financial security and personal safety to provide services to those in need. Even in the corporate world, courageous entrepreneurs are often willing to sacrifice comfortable careers, turn down prestigious positions, or risk certain success when they seize on an opportunity with good potential. Occasionally, we'll even hear about politicians who sacrifice reelection hopes for a good cause, often facing ridicule and opposition for their selfless decisions. Whether we agree with their causes or not doesn't seem to matter. If we look hard enough, we are sure to find advocates, leaders and anonymous helpers all around us.

    All these examples have two things in common: personal sacrifice and service to others. In each example we see how sacrificing their own needs for security, success, and society often leads to a life of peace and purpose. Instead of protecting or defending themselves, they turn their attention to others and work selflessly toward an ideal. They are often able to be honest and straightforward, selfless and loving, even if those around them are corrupt and selfish. Instead of being trapped by worries about success or prestige, they seem content with a purpose-driven life. They meet ridicule and adversity with grace and dignity, so their efforts inspire others. For many of these people, there's no need to keep score or compete because personal success isn't the goal. These amazing people face impossible odds, often with little success, and they continue to push forward long after most reasonable folks would have surrendered.

Why can't we apply this same approach to our chaotic lives? As parents of a special needs child, we don't have to look further than our own families and friends to find good opportunities for service. Every day, we face threats to our security, social needs, and success ... and so do our children. If we can sacrifice those unreasonable demands we make on others for security, social concerns, and success, we might better turn our attention toward serving our children, our family, and our community. If we can do this, we might finally find a sense of usefulness. More importantly, we can escape the burden of our own problems by helping others—especially our children—overcome theirs.

Every time we put aside our own needs to help someone else fulfill theirs, we will feel a sense of relief. It is counterintuitive but true. If we help others to find security, we will be more secure regardless of our situation. If we assist a person who's struggling with ambitions, we will be less driven by our own. If we can help our children to build social tools, we will become more open and free. By sacrificing our own needs to help others with theirs, we will finally feel peace and a true purpose despite adverse conditions.

This is a simple but drastic solution, so why should we try it? The answer is simple. Although our motives are good, a life spent fighting to get our own way, while defending ourselves and our children at all costs, doesn't work. It puts us in conflict with everyone around us and leads us to frequent moments of crisis. Most importantly, it is a losing battle. Being in conflict with everybody and everything around us hasn't helped us to find the security, success, or happiness that we were pursuing. Even worse, we were setting a bad example for our special needs children, who are also struggling with their own security, success, and happiness issues.

Finding a solution to those problems in our lives is the best way to help our children find answers that work for them. When a child is struggling with their own plans and expectations, who is better suited to show them the way out than a parent who has already risen above their own petty ambitions? When a child is isolated because of their condition, who is better suited to bring comfort and companionship than a parent who has come to terms with isolation? When a child is facing a life of insecurity—emotionally, mentally, and financially—who is better able to show them how to find peace than a parent that has found it themselves? Even though we had good motives, trying to help our children to cope with insecurity, relationships, and aspirations without being able to solve those issues in our own lives is like a drowning lifeguard struggling to save a drowning swimmer.

Once we've solved our own daily crisis, we can finally become a good mentor for our children. We can finally be honest and straightforward with our children, admitting that we struggle, too. We can better mentor them with personal examples of our successes and failures. We can be loving, even to those who are unloving toward us, and we find that we are finally able to be unselfish, even when it seems that others are snatching everything they can get out of life. Through the discipline of our inventory, we can become practiced at making honest, straightforward, selfless, and loving decisions despite our own insecurities, our failed plans and routines, or our struggles with other people and society. We will finally understand the firefighter who rushes into a burning building because we will no longer be in crisis, and that will free us to be better parents and better people.

At the end of each day, we can still look for those moments that got away from us, and we can see how our crisis manifested into bad behavior. We can identify those security issues, spoiled expectations, and social pressures that we missed, so that we can be better prepared for tomorrow's obstacles. As we grow in effectiveness, it will surprise us to find that there are fewer of those big moments of crisis than we once had. Instead, we begin to search out the more subtle crisis, like the silent scorn, the snub, and the simple annoyance that was never on our radar before. We begin to build on our successes rather than get overwhelmed by our failures. After a while, we commence to find that peace and purpose that we never could find before.

Nine times out of ten, we find that those security issues, spoiled expectations, and societal pressures are easy to overcome when taken one at a time. Often, we find it easy to sacrifice our own needs because we will find that most issues we face are not as important as they feel. If we deal with those minor insecurities as they pop up in our daily lives, we find that they don't pile up. As we become more aware of our unreasonable demands on ourselves and everybody else, we can stop clinging so tightly to the world around us. As we deal with those small slights, minor disagreements, and inconsequential conflicts, we begin to get a better perspective. We begin to see that everyone is plagued by these issues throughout the day, and we feel relief every time we help someone else or step out of their way. When we are better aware of those threats to our peace and security, we are more capable of making better decisions than we made when we reacted blindly to threats we didn't even understand.

Of course, we will still have to act if a real crisis presents itself. When I became consciously aware of my physical insecurity during my son's meltdowns, I was able to seek out expert help. I was able to develop healthy strategies like safeholds and de-escalation techniques that served me and my son well during his moments of crisis. By learning to differentiate between physical dangers and emotional dangers, I became better able to defend myself appropriately without retaliating, fighting, and arguing.

Sacrifice and service may not be an option with certain perils, but we can make better decisions in these situations if we are not driven by crisis. A life-and-death situation certainly can't be ignored. There are also many problems that might not be life or death but can still pose a serious risk to us or our families. Evictions, food insecurities, important medical appointments, chronic health problems, and psychological strains must be handled immediately, but we find ourselves better equipped when we are not carrying the weight from all the other problems that swirl around in our minds and keep us up at night.

There are certainly times when we must clear our schedule or make a prompt decision to act, but a parent on the brink of crisis will almost certainly fail when these situations arise. We will be unable to make sound decisions if we are already overwhelmed by our emotions. That is why it is so important, especially for a parent of a special needs child, that we stay as far from crisis as possible during the course of daily living. We will face life-threatening and serious situations more often than most parents, so we can't afford to be on the brink of a meltdown when one presents itself. The good news is that most threats aren't at this serious or life-and-death level.

Most of the problems we face are normal, everyday issues that might be complicated by disability or more plentiful because of the disability. Even though these problems aren't life-threatening, they will often feel like it to an emotionally overwrought parent. Without a regular self-evaluation, most of us won't be aware of security issues as they pile up until they prove too hard to handle. We won't notice the many decisions we make throughout the day or see how they change as problems begin to accumulate. If we cannot be honest with ourselves, how can we expect to be honest and straightforward with those around us?

If we are not consciously aware of our decisions and why we make them, it shouldn't surprise us that we become more manipulative, less loving, and more selfish as the day progresses. Then, still unaware that we have any emotional problems at all, we encounter our child in distress and react poorly. At the end of the day we look back on those meltdowns as a moment of crisis, but if we are being honest, we had been building toward that moment throughout our day. Sure, it takes a lot of time and effort to become aware of these pressures before they spin out of control, but it's worth it to avoid the damage caused by emotional crises.

Most of us are unaware of the threats around us until they become dire, but they are still affecting us throughout the day. Plans shift, and we adjust. We face a small money issue or physical threat, and we modify our behavior. We run into a problem with a coworker or boss, and we act accordingly. Slowly, almost imperceptibly, we grow annoyed, uncomfortable, or nervous. As our problems begin to accumulate, we begin to feel out of balance. This is the state of mind that usually precedes a moment of crisis. We weren't even aware that problems were piling up before the tipping point.

Becoming aware of mounting problems before they become critical should be our main objective. If this inventory becomes a part of our daily lives, we gain great insight into our relationship with the world around us. It enables us to better utilize those coping mechanisms that we already have. If we can become better aware of mounting problems, we can better incorporate those medical, psychological, religious, and physical resources into our lives in a more proactive manner. More importantly, a better understanding of our security issues, social pressures, and unreasonable demands provides us with an escape from the horrible isolation that we have felt.

More than most people, parents of special needs children find it hard to discuss their problems because few people understand our unique struggles. How often do we find a sympathetic family member or friend trying to offer advice only to drive home the point that they just don't understand the unique problems posed by our family's special need? No matter how hard they try, they can't identify with our struggles. Even specialists and teachers often fall short when it comes to understanding our daily lives. Strategies that work in the highly structured classroom can become oppressive or unsustainable in the home. Medical professionals who have devoted their lives to treating our children's conditions can often lack the real-world experience to fully understand the stress that can pervade a home.

On the other hand, everyone has experience with insecurity, overwhelming plans, unrealized expectations, and social problems, so focusing on these underlying issues with a sympathetic friend can lead to a more fruitful discussion than engaging in finger-pointing at things outside our control. It is easier to find common ground about a scheduling conflict than sharing the specific details of the conflict. Were our ambitions too high? Did we fail to prepare enough? What happens when our expectations aren't met? Are we controlling too much? Too little? How do other people solve these issues?

We may find that these sympathetic friends have faced similar emotional problems, and we may find that they have solutions that could work for us despite the differences in our situations. It is less important that they understand the details of our fight than it is to discuss coping mechanisms and strategies. Learning ways that our sympathetic friends have overcome their insecurities, spoiled plans, or societal pressures can help us to find solutions that might work for us. By focusing on solutions rather than rehashing problems, we will be better prepared for that next moment of crisis.

Conversations about security issues and relationship issues can be just as helpful. When we specifically see how we can get trapped by our social needs, we can develop solutions that work with other people. If paralyzed by our self-esteem, we can get helpful feedback from family or friends who have faced similar problems. If, on the other hand, we are constantly looking for prestige, social standing, or that pat on the back, we can find examples of how others have faced those issues. More importantly, they may have figured out ways to solve them in their lives, and that might help with our own situations.

This is the path to peace and purpose. We can measure our

progress by the decisions we make as we approach those moments of crisis. As we become more self-aware, more disciplined, and more practiced, we begin to rise above our emotions to make better decisions in those trying moments. Anybody can be self-sacrificing, tolerant and loving when people are acting the way we expect. The most despicable criminal is nice to their friends. The key to good living is found in the way we act when things aren't going our way. That's a common state in a special needs home.

It is a reasonably simple solution, but it isn't easy. It takes practice and steady improvement. But every time that we make the decision to sacrifice our own needs to serve our children, we will find relief. When we lay aside our own security issues to help someone else with theirs, we become more secure in ourselves. Instead of trying to boost our self-esteem by focusing on ourselves and those closest to us, we can engage in estimable actions by focusing on other people. To the extent that we can stop trying to force our plans, we can try to help others fulfill theirs. In doing so, we find peace and purpose.

It was clear that, in order to help our children navigate these issues in their lives, we would have to first solve them in our own lives. During preflight instructions, flight attendants advise passengers to secure their own masks before attempting to help their children. They point out that an unconscious parent would be of little help to the child next to them. The same reasoning can be applied to our emotional lives. Our own experience shows that we can be of no help to our children in crisis if we are in crisis, too.

We will need to be more conscious about the decisions in front of us and more disciplined with our choices. After identifying the moment of crisis, we must identify those unconscious drivers that made us vulnerable. First, we look for security issues we were facing—financial, emotional, and mental. Next, we search out those social pressures that we may or may not have noticed. Finally, we uncover those plans—conscious and unconscious—that were driving our decisions. At the start, a mental checklist probably won't be enough. Putting pen to paper will help us see these issues clearly, and the time spent will be worthwhile.

Only then can we begin to practice better decision-making. We cannot rely on our instincts because a parent in crisis can usually admit that this way of living hasn't worked. We have to force ourselves to be honest and straightforward, unselfish and loving. This is impossible to do when driven by crisis, so we need to be more aware of threats to our security, relationships, plans, and expectations before we face a tipping point. We have to understand our vulnerabilities if we are going to make better decisions in that state.

As we become more conscious of the underlying issues that we face throughout our day, we can begin to find strategies to resolve those issues before the crisis hits. Free from crisis, we will be in a better position to help our children when their inevitable crisis hits. By understanding these issues in ourselves, we will be

# THE BALANCING ACT

better able to identify them for our children. By solving these problems in ourselves, we will be better able to help our children find a solution that works for them. Through our experience, we will be able to mentor them through their challenges. We will become better parents, especially during trying times.

As parents in crisis, we should never lose sight of the ultimate goal. If a parent learns to identify the many unique challenges that plague them daily, they can rise above the chaos and crisis. The goal is not to eliminate those very real threats to our security, aspirations, and social lives. The goal is to find harmony, peace, and purpose despite those threats. Special needs children, and their families, are the most vulnerable people in today's society, so learning to live, grow, and love under these circumstances should be our main purpose.

Parents are the moral compass for any family. A peaceful parent is honest and straightforward, selfless, and loving. For a parent in crisis, achieving this is impossible. But, through sacrifice and service, we can keep a family on course for a happy and meaningful existence. Calm heads will prevail.

# CHAPTER FOUR

*Safety and Security: What Worries You, Masters You*

---

Few people are as vulnerable as special needs children, and few people struggle with security issues as much as the special needs family. Sometimes, it seems that our whole lives are consumed with safety issues and vulnerabilities. As soon as we start to review our days, we begin to draw a direct line between those moments of crisis and some form of underlying insecurity. Often, we aren't even aware of the many ways that these threats affect our daily decisions, but it doesn't take long, if we are honest, to see how these security issues negatively affect our emotional well-being. Even when a crisis is sparked by some other cause, like a disagreement or a disappointment, there is usually an underlying safety or security issue that has already driven us right to the brink of crisis.

## SAFETY AND SECURITY

Of course, special needs families aren't the only ones to experience insecurity. Security issues are universal. Every living thing deals with threats to its safety and challenges to its survival. Fish seek safety in the river, a place where they can find shelter and food while avoiding predators. Many animals seek safety in herds while they look for water, food, and a mate. Even plants have survival instincts that affect the way they survive and flourish. Tree roots dig for food and water, while branches stretch toward the sunlight. Small plants aren't the first to bloom each spring by accident. They race to flower and reproduce before the forest canopy blocks out the sun. Humans are no exception. Solving safety and security issues is necessary for us to bloom and flourish, too. Of course, this poses a unique challenge to special needs children and their families.

Security issues are impossible to overcome by sheer determination. Ignoring them doesn't make them go away, nor does attacking them head-on. The more a person works to satisfy this need for security, the bigger the threats appear. We try to arrange the world around us and our child in order to control costs, avoid physical triggers, and keep away anything that would upset our fragile state. But the more we try to control our environment, the more it spirals out of control. The more we focus on avoiding threats, the more threats we seem to encounter.

By their very nature, disabilities complicate daily living. People with physical disabilities often require accommodations and modifications just to accomplish simple daily tasks. People with mental disabilities may require assistance with even the most mundane decisions. People with emotional disabilities might have to summon extraordinary resources just to carry out a simple routine. As parents of children with disabilities, we become so used to these obstacles that, on the surface, they begin to feel as comfortable as a favorite outfit. Overcoming obstacles usually becomes our greatest strength, but those same obstacles often lead us to our worst moments. As we carefully review those moments of crisis that crop up throughout our day, we find that insecurity issues lurk behind everything that we encounter and weigh on every decision that we make. Subtly, subconsciously, we find that insecurity dominates our lives.

At times, threats motivate us. Like cornered cats, we come out swinging, fighting off obstacles to our children and building up fortresses to protect them physically and emotionally. We juggle multiple tasks and take on second jobs just to make ends meet. We are constantly advocating for our children's special needs, and we often craft complex daily plans designed to protect them from the many threats they face. Driven by good intentions, we find ourselves in conflict with everyone and everything around us as we defend and protect them. Even though a crisis wasn't directly sparked by some threat to daily living, we must concede that insecurity, coupled with fatigue and conflict, constantly drives us toward crisis.

## SAFETY AND SECURITY

At other times, we find that security threats and safety issues have the opposite effect. Confronted by some threat, we become paralyzed. Perhaps financial, physical, and mental pressures push us to give up entirely. Or, overwhelmed by so many vulnerabilities, we decide to lock ourselves up like prisoners in our own homes just to avoid the trouble of venturing out in public. Applications for assistance stay blank, chores are pushed off, and simple repairs go unfinished. Parents of special needs children often find themselves stretched to the breaking point. It shouldn't surprise anyone when we retreat into our shells like a turtle in danger. The cruel truth is that insecurities drive special needs parents at certain times, and paralyze us at others.

It doesn't help that the normal tools for coping with insecurities—like hope and confidence about the future—fall flat in special needs homes. For most special needs families there is no light at the end of the tunnel. When I learned that my son's disability was incurable and permanent, it added to every worry that I had about his future ... and mine. His condition meant that he'd probably struggle with self-sufficiency throughout his life. Fully independent living might never be a realistic goal. Every financial problem loomed larger because of my son's uncertain future. It's a common and justifiable fear among special needs parents. How will our children survive once we're gone? If there are no siblings, those fears can amplify.

Finding balance under these conditions seems impossible,

but that's because we have been focusing on the wrong end game. We have been trying to eliminate insecurity from our lives and the lives of our children, but this puts us in a common state of turmoil and conflict. Nowhere in history has any person been able to fully free themselves from all of their safety and security concerns. Instead, we should have been searching for a way to find peace and purpose despite those ongoing insecurities. We must find a way to make decisions that aren't fueled by fear or desperation. That requires a better understanding of the threats we face and a firm resolution to make the right decision no matter what the cost to ourselves. If we can free ourselves from emotional decision-making, then we will make better decisions. If we can shrug off the weight of these insecurities, we will be closer to finding balance and peace.

Every parent envisions a future with fully independent children, but this may be unrealistic, especially with the vulnerabilities that come with a special need. However, a parent who has learned to live in an insecure world is much better suited to pass that knowledge on to their children than a parent who falsely believes that they can be so self-sufficient that they need no outside help. A parent who has tools for overcoming insecurities is better equipped to help an insecure child with special needs. A better purpose might be to help them find the tools that they need to be peaceful and happy in a world that seems stacked against them. Then, with determination, effort, and luck, our children may

## SAFETY AND SECURITY

find the safety, success, and social lives that they deserve ... with a little help and direction from us.

It is important to note that history is peppered with examples of disabled people contributing at the highest levels of society. Franklin D. Roosevelt overcame a physical disability to become president of the United States long before Congress had drafted any laws to protect disabled citizens. Stephen Hawking made most of his academic contributions after being diagnosed with his debilitating neurological disease. Winston Churchill and King George VI overcame lifelong speech disorders to lead the British people. Despite deafness and blindness, Helen Keller graduated college, traveled the world, and became a noted leader for causes ranging from women's suffrage and labor rights to worldwide peace and social reform. Some experts even conclude that great thinkers like Albert Einstein fell somewhere on the autism spectrum. Throughout history, people with disabilities have overcome great obstacles to make important contributions in almost every known field. All of them were insecure, yet all of them developed the skills and support to overcome those vulnerabilities. That's just as true for people without disabilities.

Most of us make decisions every day without realizing how much our choices are influenced by insecurity, but for a parent in crisis this can be dangerous. As our emotions build, decisions become more irrational, erratic, and wild. Knee-jerk reactions fueled by emotion can have serious consequences for us and our children. When angry, we retaliate. When afraid, we may shut down. At the very least, we become so wrapped up in ourselves that we cannot possibly offer solutions to our children.

Second-guessing past decisions becomes an art form. Weighing current difficulties with past mistakes becomes a way of life until our perspective becomes so warped that we become overwhelmed. In order to thrive as a family, parents must learn to understand and solve their many insecurities, so that the whole family can make better choices.

Our daily review holds the answer to understanding ourselves and those emotional decisions. Once we've identified a moment of crisis, we can begin to search out the underlying security issues that may have influenced our decisions. Even if insecurity wasn't the tipping point, we quickly find that those physical, mental, emotional, and financial obstacles have often pushed us to the edge. We are conscious of some threats, but we will certainly find that we are ignorant of most. How can we possibly have good judgment when we don't fully understand a problem? By carefully reviewing each moment of crisis, we can become more aware of security threats long before they overwhelm us. This self-awareness is the true object of our daily reviews.

Security issues are often complex, and specific threats vary from person to person. To better understand insecurities faced by special needs families, we can start with a well-established list of common human threats. Late last century, the United Nations

## SAFETY AND SECURITY

undertook a worldwide study on the effects of insecurity at the international level. They found that unchecked security issues at the local level begin to overlap and grow exponentially, eventually leading to an international crisis. Insecurity is a common spark for war, poverty, famine, and loss of lives. The UN study culminated with a list of seven types of insecurity that plagued all nations, big and small: economic, personal, food, environmental, health, community and political insecurities.[1] The belief is that, in order to make better policy decisions, it is important to understand these seven elements of insecurity.

This same process can be applied to our individual lives. With a better understanding of these seven factors, and the way that they complicate our decisions, we can learn to make better choices. By understanding our insecurities, we will be able to make decisions that are free from fear or emotion. It seems counterintuitive, but accepting our insecurities and focusing on helping others (like our children) overcome their feelings of insecurity, is the best way to feel secure.

Economic insecurities are the easiest to recognize because financial independence is one of the most elusive goals for any special needs child. According to a 2020 study by the US Census Bureau, approximately one in four disabled adults lives in poverty in the United States, and that number is growing. Even more disheartening is that disabled people are disproportionately poor. According to the study, people reporting disabilities represented just 7.4 percent of the total population (aged eighteen to sixty-four), but this group represented 17.6 percent of the total population in poverty.[2]

Unfortunately, the 2020 report focused solely on disabled adults. Very few studies focus on families with disabled children, but when one member of a family has a special need, it affects everyone else in the household, especially the parents. A 1998 study by the National Disability Institute showed that approximately 28 percent of disabled children aged three to twenty-one were living in poverty,[3] and those numbers have almost certainly increased over the last decades as our understanding of the link between disability and poverty has increased. Most experts agree that families with disabled children are more likely to face economic problems, but no special needs parent requires a study to prove it. Financial strain is the biggest reality of daily living.

Living with a disability in the household often creates a number of financial dilemmas. On an almost daily basis, parents are confronted with situations that require short- and long-term sacrifices for the family's financial welfare. Everyday costs, like childcare, can be exponentially higher if one-on-one childcare or other modifications are needed. Disability creates extra costs for the household, such as medical bills, transportation expenses, special diets, and other accommodations. These obstacles can be numerous and expensive. Work pressures are increased as a parent tries to juggle schedules and doctor's appointments. Every

## SAFETY AND SECURITY

promotion at work has to be weighed against its impact on the home, so parents are often confronted with the prospect of working more flexible, lower-paying jobs in order to strike a balance between paychecks and parenting responsibilities. Worry, jealousy, and frustration often simmer beneath the surface, waiting for the next problem that might finally spark an emotional or financial crisis.

The isolation this leads to can be crippling. It often feels like nobody understands our unique financial hurdles, and useful advice is often too costly or difficult to find. The special needs family often feels as if they are on the precipice of financial ruin, so striking a balance between security, social issues, plans, and expectations can feel overwhelming. Even worse is the feeling that nobody can possibly understand our unique concerns or the decisions that we're forced to make. Feelings that we are misunderstood create even more loneliness, and that increases relationship problems. Success often feels so impossible that these fears threaten almost every plan and expectation for the future. In this state of imbalance, a moment of crisis is practically inevitable.

Balancing work schedules with our children's health needs can create job instability. This can lead to more fears about job loss, more financial worries, and greater concerns about benefits like health care and personal time. Taking a lower-paying job that affords flexibility might offer short-term benefits to our schedules and routines, but it makes those long-term financial fears worse.

Committing to long-term goals creates challenges for our current schedules, routines, and social lives. Even when there are two parents in a household, every advantage for one parent seems to create distinct disadvantages for the other. At times, striking a balance feels impossible.

The good news is that parents may feel this financial burden more than their special needs child. The concept of money came much later to my son, but I had been struggling with every financial decision for years. I had scaled back our lives, our home, and our purchases. I had become accustomed to prioritizing every need, and it sometimes took months or years to save up for items that others seemed to purchase on a whim.

Without knowing it, my decision-making process had been presenting my son with lessons about patience, charity, and unselfishness. My example helped shape his own perceptions about material security. At times, I felt overwhelmed by financial fears, but I learned to make decisions despite that fear, and those lessons weren't lost by my son. By the time he finally understood the concept of money, he had already grown into an unselfish young man who made few demands for toys, designer clothes, costly clubs or vacations. We had both learned to live within our means, manage our meager finances, and stretch our money further than most people can dream of doing without feeling as if we were making sacrifices at all. It wasn't easy. Financial fears sometimes threatened to overwhelm me, but through my daily review I learned to spot the

## SAFETY AND SECURITY

threats, prioritize them, and cope with them.

Of course, security issues aren't just measured in dollars and cents, but most insecurities often overlap with financial issues. Every special needs family has some sort of medical, physical, or psychological issue that is inescapable. In addition, we often encounter unique bureaucratic obstacles with issues like health care, government assistance, or community resources. Taken separately, any one of these issues can be overwhelming, but in a special needs home problems overlap and complicate each other. Also, underlying every one of these insecurities is a chronic financial trouble that is fairly universal, along with all of the environmental challenges that poverty creates. There is a price tag associated with every security issue, but they often impact our time and thinking more than our wallets.

Let's take a look at each one of these elements individually:

Many personal security issues pose a real physical threat to parent and child. Living with a disability carries all the typical challenges of daily living, but it also creates unique barriers specific to each special need. At almost every stage of his development, new and unexpected problems would flare up in my son, resulting in new temper tantrums and different meltdowns. Emotions, left unchecked, would build quickly into rage-filled attacks that I would be forced to fend off. Parents of autistic children are often required to become expert at safeholds and self-defense, often putting our own bodies and minds at risk to secure the safety of our children, along with anyone close by when a tantrum explodes.

Once, at a family gathering, my son became so overwhelmed by the simple singing of a birthday song that we had to make a quick exit. I was so focused on his safety that I didn't realize the relentless flurry of punches he was throwing at my head while I was trying to get him into the car. Eventually, my vision blurred and my knees grew rubbery. I barely felt the hands of two family members as they caught me before my fall. This wasn't a singular occurrence. There were times when it took multiple people to restrain my son at school, but in our home that responsibility fell squarely on my shoulders. For years, my scratched and bruised face recorded those efforts.

Although physical attacks are common with my son's condition, this level of physical threat isn't common in every special needs home. But in every special needs home there are physical challenges, emotional obstacles and legitimate worries that, over time, can lead to frustration or fatigue. We are frequently called upon to provide assistance for physical limitations, de-escalate emotional turmoil, and provide services for daily living. These efforts, happily provided, can place us in a chronic state of insecurity that draws us ever closer to that eventual moment of crisis. Safety issues are complicated by other physical, mental, and emotional threats we encounter in the course of everyday living. Understanding these personal insecurities is crucial if we are going to develop better strategies to deal with them.

## SAFETY AND SECURITY

Special needs families can often become so overwhelmed by personal insecurity and hardship issues that they don't even realize it until it's too late. Parents wake each morning with a sort of emotional hangover from yesterday's stress that isn't easily shaken off. As they go through their day, they encounter other problems—sometimes big ones, sometimes small ones. Inevitably, a stressed parent will finally confront a financial obstacle, a physical threat, or some other form of emotional turmoil that can prove too much to handle. The emotional hangover is just the first in each day's string of red lights.

Sometimes, there is an emotional toll paid for physical security issues. If a child has violent tantrums, such as my own, it can pose a real physical threat to anyone close by. Paralyzed by this fear, everyone in the household is forced to walk on eggshells, trying to avoid anything that might trigger an outburst. At times, parents may even be forced to protect themselves—physically and mentally—from their own children. This is compounded by a child's persistent physical and mental security issues in almost every public situation, along with the fatigue parents feel as they constantly try to redirect and protect their child. The constant need to avert a crisis becomes its own security crisis. Loneliness and isolation are common results for families with special needs children, and they often bring forth a whole wave of social insecurities.

There are other issues, like food insecurity, that can create chronic problems in our daily lives. At the international level, food insecurity is often measured by hunger issues or limited access to high-quality food, but it can take on a broader definition in a special needs home. Special needs children often have special diets, limited palates, or other food issues that create stress in the household. Often, parents are forced to cook separate meals or make other drastic compromises in order to secure the food necessary for daily living. These food issues can influence everyday plans, adding emotional insecurities that can influence everyday decisions.

As an autistic child, my son's food issues were legendary. He only eats certain foods, and his choices are very limited. Brands matter. Preparation matters. If the right food isn't available, he would rather go hungry than try something new. This always presents one more hurdle to cross no matter where we go. Whether it's a regular school day, a special event, or a weeklong vacation, food issues must always be taken into account when making plans. Sometimes, I've decided to skip events and vacations altogether because of my son's food issues. At the very least, it added stress any time we left our home. At times, it paralyzed me.

My family's issues aren't unique. One school year, my son's classroom worked food issues into the curriculum since it was such a common problem. My son's plan focused on a plain hamburger with no bun, no seasoning, and no condiments, since that was a fairly common food at many events like picnics and birthday parties. We tracked his progress all year. He smelled it. He touched

## SAFETY AND SECURITY

it with his finger. He touched it with his tongue. He put it in his mouth without spitting it out. He even took a bite. That summer, at a Fourth of July picnic, we finally had a chance to test the results. He watched the burger cook on the grill. We placed it on a clean plate. My son refused it.

Popcorn, crackers, and cookies have all served as comfort foods at various times, and my son demanded these snacks at regular times or during stressful events. The brand mattered so much that, I once tried hiding a store brand cracker in the name-brand packaging, and he refused to try it. These sorts of problems are more common in special needs homes than people might think. Sometimes, a parent might find it easier to skip an event because of the cost and preparation required. This, of course, leads to more isolation, which leads to more emotional and mental insecurity.

On the other hand, we were lucky. Many children have severe allergies or medical issues that raise the level of stress and costs exponentially, but all food issues—big or small—add unique stresses that most parents never have to face. A friend of mine once filled an entire closet with a particular snack cake that was soon to be discontinued. Luckily, it went back into production before she ran out of it. Who would think that a discontinued junk food would create such a desperate food security issue? With many special needs parents, these worries are common.

Money problems, personal issues, and food demands are just the tip of the iceberg when it comes to insecurities in the special needs home. There are environmental factors that arise from necessary modifications, accommodations, and needs. Poverty and money issues can complicate this problem. It can often feel impossible to find a secure environment for our children. Sometimes, special needs families live in a sort of self-imposed exile just to be able to handle the many environmental factors that pose a risk to our children's physical, emotional, or mental well-being. It amazed me how many moments of crisis could be traced to some sort of environmental insecurity. Every time we moved to a different environment, there was added stress. Controlling my son's environment helped me justify some of my worst behaviors. Every time I entered a room, I would scan for threats and act accordingly. To avoid meltdowns, I could easily rationalize manipulative behaviors like scripting conversations with my child, overcorrecting other people's behaviors, and placing barriers between others and my child. I could interrupt a conversation at any time. I could leave a gathering suddenly, with no notice or explanation. To me, these behaviors appeared honest and straightforward, selfless, and loving, but to everyone else it must have appeared manipulative and self-centered. This is the way that insecurity can transform a typically rational parent into an overbearing know-it-all. This is a major way that a parent in crisis loses perspective.

It is easy to see how health issues can pose serious challenges. Scheduling doctor's visits, securing necessary medical

## SAFETY AND SECURITY

equipment, or finding qualified experts can create such a drain on the family's resources that many special needs families choose to forgo all those little extras, like vacations and outings, that make family living so satisfying. Special needs children, by definition, have challenges to their physical, mental, or emotional health that have to be taken into consideration when making even the most mundane decisions. It helps to talk about our problems before making decisions, but finding the right person is critical. It should be someone who has enough emotional distance that their feedback won't be biased by their perspective. Sometimes, we just need another person to listen without offering guidance. If so, we should be clear about that before the conversation begins. Most people will be happy to help when approached with clarity.

Although great strides have been made to include special needs children in schools and social circles, community insecurities can also be overwhelming. More and more communities are developing special needs outlets, from art groups and sports teams to social clubs and buddy systems, but community events are often the first thing sacrificed in a struggling household. Also, most community supports are nonprofit and run by volunteers. These organizations often struggle with funding, communication, long-term consistency, or survival. Still, the effort necessary to volunteer or to participate is always worthwhile as long as parents can stay open-minded and cooperative.

One of the hardest insecurities to overcome is political

because special needs people are often among the least represented by government and least able to advocate for themselves. Even when help is available, that can create another level of insecurity in a battle with red tape and bureaucracy. Something as straightforward as pursuing necessary accommodations or public assistance through government programs can create headaches and pressure. For example, securing disability and health-care coverage often requires that someone is incapable of working. Yet most anti-poverty programs carry a work requirement. This often creates a dilemma between struggling in the labor market or leaving it altogether. Even low-paying jobs can jeopardize programs like food stamps or the earned income tax credit. Often, neither option is a good one.

In some cases, avoiding the emotional and physical strain that comes from applications and red tape, an overwhelmed parent might opt to decline necessary help. The hard reality is that it doesn't always matter if a mentally disabled person works with reduced benefits or doesn't work in order to receive full benefits. Neither decision will likely change the fact that a special needs child is likely to be unable to escape poverty. Even in the unlikely scenario that money can be saved or assets can be built, that would only jeopardize future benefits or trigger repayment of past benefits unless a parent sets up complex legal measures ... which adds the additional stress of legal costs.

To list all of the insecurities that a special needs family will

## SAFETY AND SECURITY

encounter is impossible. Every disability and every household will encounter unique challenges based on their individual circumstances. Financial issues, food issues, health issues, and personal issues are fairly universal, but they will manifest differently in every family. By reviewing our moments of crisis, parents can learn to identify security issues, prioritize them, and deal with them. Some might be easily solved. Others may linger for years. Some insecurities might be permanent.

All problems can be lessened by discussing them with people who understand, and this is the biggest challenge for special needs parents. It often seems impossible to find somebody who might fully understand us. As a result, isolation itself becomes one of the biggest insecurities in a special needs home. We get unsolicited advice from well-meaning friends or family that only proves to show how little they understand our situations. We learn to hide our problems from others. We sidestep discussions about money, and we feel even more set apart from others. Loneliness, misunderstanding, and isolation are common in a special needs home.

The first step toward overcoming insecurities is to identify the threats around us, but the second step is to discuss them so we can divorce our decisions from our emotions. Reviewing our own moments of crisis begins to paint a picture for us of how insecurities multiply, overlap, and grow. Perhaps a money problem popped up when we were already struggling with accommodation or fighting off a child's attack. That might have been the final straw, igniting a crisis that fueled a bad parenting moment. Understanding these threats and the way we react to them can give us great insight into ourselves and our children. If we can identify these threats before they become a moment of crisis, we might be able to make better decisions. Who knows? We might be able to avoid a crisis altogether.

Insecurity isn't discussed openly in modern society, but if we search for an understanding person—perhaps one who has overcome insecurity themselves—we can rise above it. Finding the right person to talk to might not be as hard as we think. All parents feel isolated at times. All parents worry about their children's security needs and the uncertainties of the future. All parents have struggled with finding resources to address a problem. Do not compare situations. Discuss the similarities. That means we should focus on the feelings, not the disabilities, the facts, or the specifics. Solving our emotional problem is often more important than solving the underlying financial or physical obstacle.

The good news is that finding someone who will understand us is not as difficult as we have presumed. Security issues are universal. Others may not understand the frustration of a unique money problem, but most people have experienced their own money problems. At some point, everybody has dealt with a financial problem, whether they are incredibly poor or exceptionally wealthy. Even the most affluent people have feelings of isolation that stem from a belief that nobody understands them. Everyone has a tendency to be skeptical of others and to keep money problems to themselves, and that distrust of others is common to people across the financial spectrum.

If we look hard enough, we will be able to identify people to talk about other insecurity issues, too, because everyone has faced insecurity at one point or another. Who hasn't felt personally threatened at some time in their lives? It might be harder to identify with someone over a food issue, but every parent has felt bogged down, trying to prepare for the unexpected. It shouldn't be hard to find people who struggled with their environment, health issues, or red tape—if we honestly search for them. Sure, their experiences might have been different, but we will find that they do understand the feelings behind the insecurities. How did they deal with it? Talking about our common feelings and reactions, along with the coping mechanisms that work and don't work, can help us to gain a better perspective to make better decisions—even in crisis.

We will usually find friends and family members happy to share their experiences when we approach them. In those rare instances when we need someone who understands a person with special needs, we will find them, too, if we keep an open mind. Teachers and paraprofessionals are good resources. They have usually encountered similar problems with a wide variety of students, and they've often received training on concepts like de-escalation techniques and safeholds. They are often willing to pass on their knowledge when appropriate. At the very least, open communication can help coordinate and reinforce techniques between school and home environments.

Psychologists, doctors, social workers, religious leaders, and police often have experience dealing with security threats. I had a family member who worked in the prison system, and his insight into personal safety issues proved helpful during the preschool era. I had another family member who worked with special needs students, and I found that some of her strategies could be used successfully in our home. No matter who we decide to talk to, it helps if it's someone who has learned to deal with these sorts of personal issues in their personal lives or professions.

When we find someone to talk to, steer away from discussions about disabilities or circumstances because that can lead to differences and misunderstandings. Instead, talk to another parent about the ways they mentor their children to deal with insecurities. Try to find common ground. Discuss how insecurities affect daily routines or expectations. Touch on how insecurities affect relationships and self-esteem. If the person you are talking to has found a solution that worked, consider it. If their attempts have failed, learn from them. Security issues are faced by every family and every person—regardless of their economic status. In this way, special needs homes are no different.

There is no blanket solution for security issues because different people may react differently in the same situation. One

## SAFETY AND SECURITY

person might respond in anger to a money issue, fighting to get their way. Another might turn inward, isolating into a self-esteem spiral that begins to affect every other decision they make. Facing a physical threat, one person might retaliate, while another might withdraw. Reactions can be anything from a snub to a full-blown fight. Even when the first reaction is to fight back, over time a person might begin to lose the will to engage. There's a whole spectrum of reactions, and it can change from day to day, hour to hour, or year to year. Being aware of the threats around us, learning to seek out help, communicating our problems, and taking action is the path out of insecurity.

As a parent tries to solve those everyday security issues, we seem to double our social and aspirational triggers. Driven by good intentions, we find ourselves in conflict with everybody and every circumstance around us. The more we fight to get our way, the more we seem to lose. At other times, we become so overwhelmed by potential issues that it paralyzes us, isolating us further and creating even more insecurity.

On the other hand, sacrificing security goals to focus on our children's physical, emotional, and mental needs often leads us into conflict with work, family, and friends. Once again, our security decision puts more pressure on our social lives and ambitions. Trying to solve our security problems seem to do nothing but create more social obstacles and challenges to our plans.

This is where that regular inventory of those moments of crisis begins to pay off. As parents get better at identifying their own security issues, they begin to understand the patterns present in their behaviors. Trends begin to surface. We begin to understand our reactions and how they might change depending on the type of insecurity. Money issues might paralyze us, while physical threats might be met with force. People may react differently to emotional insecurities than they do to physical ones. Eventually, we begin to understand our reactions, and the decisions we make when we are threatened. Only then, can we begin to develop solutions that work. We may not be able to sidestep every problem, but we can develop healthy coping mechanisms and better decision-making. Through practice, we can better handle those moments of crisis.

As we become more aware of our own insecurities, it becomes easier to spot them in others, especially in our special needs children. It wasn't long after I began to recognize my own insecurities that I began to see my son struggling with the same issues as me. I was consumed with economic, personal, food, environmental, health, community, and political insecurities, but so was he. Sure, our struggles manifested in different ways, but we had more in common than I thought. Often, we were competing for the same things. Sometimes my fears were echoed by his anger. Sometimes, it was the other way around. The more I understood what was driving my emotions, the more I seemed to understand what was driving his.

## SAFETY AND SECURITY

I found that my son struggled with insecurities just like any other person, but he lacked the language to understand them, discuss them, and create strategies to overcome them. Left unchecked, these insecurities grew and multiplied. Eventually, they turned to anger because that's the easiest emotion to understand. I learned that his meltdowns—and mine—were just symptoms of other, unresolved emotions. By helping him to identify feelings before they became a crisis, we could often avert the crisis altogether.

Even with an understanding of our insecurities, we may struggle to understand our child's perspective. We may be uncertain about how to approach them or identify with them. Once again, finding someone to talk to can help us to develop the best approach, and finding the right person might not be as difficult as it might seem at first.

Seek out a parent of a gifted child. You'll find that their children often face similar issues with isolation and insecurity. Like us, parents of gifted children worry that they are not giving their children all of the help that they need. They, too, worry that they don't always understand their children's needs and that they are missing opportunities. They also struggle to relate at times. These common issues are a good starting point for any healthy discussion.

Better yet, go to the source itself. Often, our biggest challenge is to understand our child's perspective, especially if the child's special need involves language. To get better insight before making an important decision, it would be beneficial to seek out someone who was labeled gifted or someone who felt different from their peers. This shouldn't be too hard to find. Everyone, at some point, has felt like an outsider. Their feelings will give great insight into your child's issues and help you identify moments from your own life. This understanding will shed light on feelings of isolation, the need to be accepted or included, and the embarrassment of being singled out. This can even help to understand the boredom or frustration felt after years of living as an outsider.

This practice will help us to identify with our own children and to draw from our own experiences. Understanding our feelings and sharing our children's perspective is necessary if we are going to better communicate with them. With an understanding of our own insecurities, we will find it easier to put into words the issues that they are struggling to understand. Armed with knowledge about ourselves, we will be able to help them to label their feelings, give voice to them, and overcome their confusion. We can offer solutions that have worked for us. We can model these solutions for our children in a simplified way that they can understand.

This approach paid immediate dividends for me and my son. Once I was able to identify with my son's insecurities, I stopped trying to solve his problems for him. Instead, I adopted a more cooperative approach. I began to see how we both reacted to physical threats or emotional triggers, and I began to identify with

## SAFETY AND SECURITY

him and his struggles. I'd use my language to label his feelings, and I'd use my own experiences to gain his confidence. Then, I'd talk about options, offer him choices, and support his decisions. Together, we learned to spot the warning signs before the meltdown.

By intervening earlier, I could better model solutions that work for me or help him develop his own coping mechanisms. By recognizing those insecurities that he might not have the language or maturity to recognize for himself, I could make better parenting decisions. It was amazing how often I could assist him through those situations that used to bewilder us.

Soon, his meltdowns over security issues—and mine—began to subside. It wasn't that we had fewer insecurities. In fact, as we became more conscious of insecurities it often felt like there were more than before. On the other hand, we began to develop better strategies and coping mechanisms, and we found that we didn't have to eliminate insecurities. We just had to deal with them. With open and honest discussion, love, and patience, we began to outgrow them.

[1] United Nations Development Program; Human Development Report; Oxford University Press, 1994.

[2] Shrider, E. et al; Income and Poverty in the United States; US Dept. of Commerce and US Census Bureau, 2020.

[3] Chilman, C., Cox, F., and Nunnally, E. Employment and Economic Problems. New Bury Park: Sage Publishing; 1988.

# CHAPTER FIVE

*Social Studies: Can't We All Just Get Along?*

---

Social problems abound in every special needs home, and mine was no exception. Since communication difficulties, social anxiety, and behavioral issues are common symptoms of my son's autism diagnosis, social issues were often front and center in our home. Communication problems were the first symptom of my son's conditions, and that kicked off a social journey that continues to challenge us. For both of us, our social issues began with his language delay.

Connecting with my son is still one of the most difficult challenges I've ever faced, and his progress has been frustratingly slow. Right from the start, his use of sounds was delayed. Eye contact was difficult for him, especially when he was young and didn't seem to acknowledge anyone else in the room. While children his age were learning to talk and play, my son was locked in a sort of prison, alternating between crying, screaming, and silence. Introducing language was such a painstaking process of trial and error for both of us, punctuated by small victories with huge setbacks. At each language hurdle, my fears grew. With each setback, my anxiety grew. Consequently, I began to question my parenting abilities, and I was having just as much trouble connecting with him as he was having with me. That thought terrified me.

We worked tirelessly on his language skills, and by the time he entered preschool, he was able to follow simple prompts and point to pictures when instructed. Sometimes, he was able to answer yes/no questions, but progress was still painfully slow. Of course, I was relieved to find that preschool gave us better access to language specialists. I had never struggled with expressing myself before, but communicating with him was like learning a new language. School specialists helped me deconstruct my speech into simpler requests, so my son could process them one at a time.

They helped me simplify everyday requests like, "Go into the kitchen and get a spoon." They pointed out that these were actually two instructions, and they explained how complex this can appear to a child struggling with language. They helped me to break it down. Over time, it became:

"Go into the kitchen."

Wait. Then ...

"Get a spoon."

Watching him grab a utensil was a great moment for us, but it took a lot more practice to do it consistently.

To avoid my son's meltdowns over his language issues, I began to jump in early to rephrase his conversations with friends or family. This is common when there are language delays. Someone would say something to him, and I would interrupt to correct their approach. As my own communication skills improved, so did my meddling. After a while, it became impossible for anybody to speak directly to my son without my involvement. With good intentions, I had created one more layer of distance between him and the world around him. Looking back on it, I was quick to share the knowledge I had learned from teachers, specialists and experts, but I was much slower to share the patience that they had shown me. Social crises can develop slowly and subtly over time, and my son's speech issues were just the tip of the iceberg. Suddenly, I was having difficulty in social situations, too.

Human beings are social creatures, so people have an inherent need to be part of a group in order to survive and thrive. Nobody fares well in isolation, not prisoners of war, not inmates in solitary confinement, not shipwrecked survivors on an uninhabited island. Studies show that people isolated from others can suffer a wide range of negative health effects. Long-term isolation and loneliness can lead to feelings of depression, paranoia, and panic. Over time, complex self-esteem issues, stress, hostilities and anxieties begin to emerge, and that can develop into chronic pessimism and social anxiety. Eventually, loneliness can lead to physical problems, too, like sleep dysfunction or compromised immune system function, and that creates a whole host of other health issues with a wide range of new social challenges. If isolation persists long enough, any declines in language or social skills can become permanent. In other words, isolation and loneliness can create an actual crisis.

Consequently, each one of us seeks opportunities for meaningful interactions and strives to find a significant place within our society. The need to be part of society is a survival instinct, and anything that threatens our ability to have meaningful social interactions and relationships can cause us to feel threatened, angry, or hurt. Socially vulnerable people react powerfully to any new threat to their social standing, and may strongly protect any friend or family member when they perceive that they are threatened. As parents of special needs children, that certainly helps explain why so many moments of crisis stem from social issues, and why we advocate so passionately to facilitate communication, inclusion, and socialization for our children. Nobody is more victimized by loneliness and isolation than a special needs child, and nobody is more afraid of the consequences of that isolation than a parent.

Despite the need for social interaction, those social encounters were the most challenging episodes for my son, especially when he was younger and language was the most challenging. These emotionally charged encounters were a common spark for his breakdowns. His struggles with language often manifested in angry tantrums. If he was forced into social situations, it often led to anxiety and more meltdowns. Any trip outside the home took preparation, courage, and extraordinary effort, yet any time we ventured into a public space, there was a good chance my son would have a crisis. This wasn't a spoiled child crying over a toy. My son's tantrums were loud, physical, and dangerous, so avoiding them was a top priority.

The only social issues that didn't spark a tantrum were the ones that dealt with social standing. He couldn't care less about his importance in a group, so meltdowns never seemed to spring out of issues with pride, self-esteem, or ego. Those were only problems for me, and those were definitely problems. Moments of crisis are easy to recognize in a special needs child because they often manifest in anger or withdrawal. They may seem to appear out of nowhere and escalate quickly. They can often materialize at inconvenient times. Sometimes, moments of crisis were just as recognizable in me, especially during the chaos of my son's tantrums.

I was constantly worried about going out in public, and those fears led to countless sleepless nights. When we were in the public spotlight, I was constantly on guard against any potential obstacle or inconvenience. Under the weight of so many ongoing social issues, one small injustice would easily tip the scales into crisis. In an instant, a parent in crisis can transform into a warrior bent on defending their child at all costs. Honesty, self-sacrifice, and respect are suddenly thrown out the window as the parent transforms into an irrational, self-serving, prized fighter. Once unleashed, there's no putting that genie back in the bottle.

I'm reminded of an incident that occurred in the courtyard of our apartment complex when my son was very young. We were crossing the lawn when we encountered a small group of neighborhood kids on the sidewalk playing basketball with a small plastic hoop. As we passed them, the ball slipped out of one kid's hands. It rolled to my son's feet, and he picked it up. Instantly, he was surrounded. The boys asked him to play, but he panicked and dropped the ball.

As I watched them return to their game, I heard one ask another, "Why did you ask him to play? I think he's *retarded*." That word and everything it implied triggered a moment of crisis in me. Luckily, my body moved slower than my mind.

I wanted to storm into the game, snatch the ball, and drag every one of those kids, kicking and screaming, to their parents' doors. I think I even took a few steps in that direction before my son caught my attention. He was just watching them, smiling. Luckily, that was enough to snap me back to reality.

I was getting ready to defend him for the way he was disrespected, but my son wasn't even aware of any slight. I was seeking revenge for an unintended injustice from a group of young children. This may have been their first encounter with a special needs child, and I had blown the opportunity to turn it into a teachable moment for them, for my son, or for me. This is the danger that social issues present. If I'm unaware of the mounting pressures, any minor incident or injury can prove to be the final straw.

A parent in crisis, in fact anybody in crisis, loses the ability to see things clearly. Emotions like anger, fear, and self-pity warp our perspective and cloud our judgment. It is often impossible to see the truth that's directly in front of us, and we overreact. That's why it's so important to be aware of our emotional challenges before they build into crisis. As we review our day, it helps to focus on those emotional moments that resulted from social issues. We begin to see that those communication issues and social challenges often spark anger, fear, jealousy, anxiety, and confusion. These feelings linger, and the social problems never really seem to go away. It's a constant emotional burden that weighs us down until we finally encounter a problem—like our child's meltdown or an injustice to us or our child—and that proves to be too much.

So many of our decisions are driven by these emotions. We begin to dread those social encounters, so we retreat further into our shells. Little by little, we wall ourselves off from the outside world. We turn down invitations. We withdraw into our homes and occupations, but that doesn't solve our anxiety. In many ways, it makes it worse. Isolation and loneliness become constant companions. Eventually, we encounter a social problem that we cannot avoid, and we find ourselves in crisis and all of our pent-up emotions spill out in the very meltdown that we were trying to avoid. It's a vicious cycle that's hard to break.

We have to overcome those social barriers if we are going to live happy and useful lives. If we employ the same solution that we applied to our security issues, we might be able to help ourselves and our children. Rather than trying to avoid the social minefield, we can embrace it as a parenting opportunity. It is counterintuitive, but sacrificing our comfort will actually make us more comfortable in public arenas.

We can't wish these problems away or overcome them by sheer determination. We can't fix the problem in our children, and we can't seem to escape the problems that result in our own lives. How do we find peace and purpose in social situations? How do we help our children adjust to a world that doesn't understand their special needs? What can we do to solve their struggles? How can we help them? These are questions that every special needs parent eventually asks themselves.

The truth is that we can't promise a world without social problems, especially when a special need—physical, mental, or emotional—becomes an additional barrier, creating a sense of separation from the world around them. On the other hand, we can help our children to understand social challenges because we have them, too. If we've learned to solve the emotional crisis in our lives, we can begin to model solutions for them. In other words, we solve social problems the same way that we solve insecurity issues: through sacrifice and service.

This doesn't mean that we sacrifice our own social needs in order to serve our children. In fact, many parents fall into this trap. So many parents sacrifice relationships, entertainment, leisure activities, and social functions in order to focus on a child's needs, but that really only creates more isolation and loneliness—the very things we are trying to avoid. When we take this path, it only leads to resentment and self-pity. What we really sacrifice is our peace of mind. In that self-imposed state of isolation, it is easy to match our children's crisis with one of our own.

We cannot model good social behavior to our children if we are withdrawing from the world. Sure, it is sometimes easier to wall ourselves up in our homes to avoid the stresses of the outside world, but this isn't sacrifice. This is self-protection. If we are going to overcome social issues, it is necessary for us to sacrifice our need to protect ourselves and instead embrace uncomfortable social situations. It sounds counterintuitive, but it isn't. The only way that we can assist our children with their social issues is to first break out of our own self-constructed prison.

Parents and children struggle with issues over self-esteem, social standing, power dynamics, and authority. Sometimes these situations build over time, but other times there is no warning whatsoever. If we aren't aware of these issues as they build, our reactions are inconsistent at best. That day in the courtyard, I was blissfully unaware of my anxiety when I stepped out my front door, and it was almost my undoing. Understanding how social issues and relationship problems manifest is critical if we are going to avoid that sudden moment of crisis, along with the emotional damage it creates in its wake.

A simple inventory before leaving the house might have better prepared me for the incident in the courtyard. I was so focused on my son's anxiety outside the house that I was totally unaware of mine, so my guard was down. Without knowing it or intending it, that perceived slight during the basketball game had pressed all the right buttons. The easiest to see, of course, was my plan for reaching our destination, but the button that they really seemed to press was the social one. When my son wasn't included in a game he didn't want to play, I took it personally. They had affected my expectations, hurt my feelings, and offended my self-esteem. It wasn't my son's problem. It was mine.

As time went on, these neighborhood kids got to know both of us when we gathered at the bus stop. Genuinely interested, they peppered me with questions about my son and his condition. They would talk to him even when he didn't respond. A few times, they were able to lure him into playing a game of catch or some other interaction. Sometimes, he'd answer their questions, but other times he'd ignore them. As for the neighborhood kids, they would wave when we passed them in the courtyard, and they always treated my son with respect. I am very grateful that my reaction during our first encounter in the courtyard was only in my head.

The truth is that parents of special needs children spend so much time focused on our plans and insecurities that we seldom account for those subtle, underlying social issues that can rise up to defeat us. Avoiding meltdowns becomes second nature. We develop a keen insight into our children's states of mind. As experts in their behaviors, we step in when we see a crisis looming. As a result, special needs parents often hover over our children in public settings. This sort of helicopter parenting is well-meaning but self-defeating. It takes away our child's chance to practice his or her communication skills in a safe environment. Without realizing it, we can be adding to their developmental delays. Instead of shielding them from triggers, a parent should be mentoring solutions and offering support.

When I adopted this approach, I found that people rarely needed my help. Often, they had more patience than I did. I had to allow others to make mistakes instead of trying to avoid them, but this was difficult for me. Even if it meant that my son would become anxious during an interaction, I had to sacrifice my own selfish concerns so that I could embrace any parenting opportunity that presented itself. Realizing that mistakes can happen, it is often better to chaperone an interaction than to direct it. It was even worth enduring my son's meltdowns once in a while to help foster communication between him and the people in our lives. An effective parent should always be available for feedback but careful about scripting other people's conversations. This isn't easy.

This new vantage point also offers other advantages. When I'm looking to help him rather than defend him, I began to notice that my son's meltdowns actually had little to do with the way other people approached him or their methods. His meltdowns were coming from his own frustration, confusion, and lack of confidence. He didn't like making mistakes any more than I did. Whenever he made one, it often sparked a tantrum.

What an epiphany to realize that both of us were struggling with perfectionism. I was trying to avoid mistakes, and he was angry any time one occurred. I realized that I could better serve my son by focusing on our shared problem and letting the experts focus on his language skills. This was another turning point in our lives. Every mistake—his or mine—was a parenting opportunity.

When a mistake happens, I turn my attention to him. I talk about my feelings, offer him choices, and discuss coping methods that I use. He may not understand everything I say, but I try to keep my words simple and watch his feedback. This approach helps both of us avoid crisis. Chapter 8 will explore this method further, but this new plan serves as a measuring stick for those social issues that plagued us. We were finally connecting to each other and the world around us, and we were doing it together.

Even when language problems don't exist, there is a wide range of social issues present in a special needs home. Communication barriers and misunderstandings are just as common when the special need is physical or emotional. Strangers may be uncertain how to approach a special needs person, or an isolated child might not always have the confidence to receive them. By taking a passive role in the social interaction, a parent will be better able to help if needed. That might mean that our plans and expectations go unfulfilled, but that's an easy sacrifice to make for our child's social welfare. Some of my favorite interactions were the unplanned and spontaneous moments I had the privilege to watch from the sidelines.

Whether or not there are language issues, socialization is a major challenge for special needs children, and it's an emotional issue for parents, too. Struggles with inclusion are common for special needs children, and that can drive the thoughts and actions of the parent. Desperate that our children have social opportunities, we become advocates, crusaders for social opportunities. Sometimes, this puts us in direct conflict with people and institutions. Many moments of crisis can be traced to inclusion issues.

Social environments can be overwhelming for children with mental and emotional challenges, but children with physical disabilities can be excluded from group activities just as often. Special needs children seem to alternate between being thrust into the spotlight or being relegated to the sidelines. Often, through nobody's fault, special needs children are excluded entirely from many social opportunities because of the need for special accommodations or modifications.

This can be a challenge for a special needs child who is already wrestling with social isolation, but it can also consume the parent. All parents become advocates for their children's needs, but this can become overwhelming in a special needs home. So much time and energy are devoted to creating social interactions. We are constantly searching for special needs groups in our neighborhoods. As we review our days, we will often find that we were so consumed with our child's social needs that it put us in some sort of conflict that drove us to crisis.

Fortunately many communities have made great strides in this area. From arts and crafts groups to sports leagues, there has been great progress in recent years toward creating activities for special needs children. Some communities offer dances, walks, movies, and other opportunities that specifically cater to the unique needs of special needs children and their families. These groups attract motivated volunteers and parents. Often, they include children without special needs as peers or partners. These are great outlets for families, especially those that struggle with communication, behavioral issues, or other obstacles that make social events challenging. Sometimes special needs children thrive in these environments. Other times, it might create additional anxieties, but this movement has opened many doors that were previously closed.

On the other hand, inclusion in ordinary, everyday events

and activities is still a struggle for people with special needs. The necessity for modifications or accommodations can be tricky at unsupervised, spontaneous events, so it's in everyday life that special needs children and their families often struggle. Parents of special needs children often feel the weight of societal pressures just as much or more than their children.

In the beginning, my choice to isolate didn't seem to cause any issues for my son. At first, it seemed to help him. Even today, my son can seem perfectly content to cut himself off from anyone outside the household. Isolation was a physical issue for him, but it was more of an emotional issue for the rest of the family. Worse, it wasn't helping my son to overcome his social disability. It was only helping to reinforce it.

As we learn to accommodate a child with emotional or mental challenges, we can finally move out of isolation and loneliness. In my family, it seemed as if my son's social struggles were the one contagious symptom of his autism. As his anxiety grew, so did mine. As his fears manifested in meltdowns, so did mine. It wasn't hard to find justification for staying home. Appeasing him was often more appealing than the prospect of leaving the house, but it left me with a chronic loneliness problem. Sacrificing my comfort helped me to overcome my social challenges and provided many opportunities to mentor my child.

Once the inclusion issue is overcome, our social problems aren't over. Once the door is open, it actually presents a whole host of other challenges as the child learns to fit into their new social group. Problems with ego, pride, and self-esteem can emerge as special needs families struggle to fit into a society that doesn't always seem to value them. Feeling different, they can struggle to find their place within a group. My son's lack of social awareness often led to boundary issues and inappropriate behavior in social situations, but even children with physical handicaps can struggle to fit in. It is common for a special needs child to feel like an outsider in most social situations, and that can lead to emotional problems for both the child and the parent.

Every social hurdle that our children face is complicated by a parent's worries about the future. Every new problem reawakens fears about the future, since we recognize the lifelong struggles that our children will face just to fit into society. Whether a child's special needs are physical, emotional or mental, they will have to overcome obstacles that most people take for granted. There will be very real challenges to finding success in those areas prized by society: education, careers, and relationships. This is a constant worry for a special needs parent, and it colors the way we see the world.

Driven by these social challenges, we advocate for our children, but this can quickly throw us out of balance if we're not careful. Parents wrestle with authority, bureaucracy, and power dynamics that can erupt into conflict as we fight for inclusion or modifications. As we focus on solving our family's social issues, the threats and obstacles become more obvious. We begin to force solutions, becoming more demanding, desperate, and disappointed. The more we struggle to balance social issues, insecurities, and solutions, the more we feel out of balance. Left unchecked, these problems grow and overlap until we find ourselves in crisis. Relationships suffer. Romance takes a back seat, and emotions build. Anger and confusion over the many obstacles we face are compounded by growing fears about the future. In this state of mind, a simple self-esteem issue, a small jealousy, or a minor injustice can spark a meltdown. It's practically inevitable.

I didn't need an inventory to recognize my son's social struggles because they are hard to miss. His social anxieties can easily overwhelm him, and his ability to understand or handle his emotions is limited. These issues make it difficult for him to thrive in larger groups—and sometimes smaller groups. Intimacy poses challenges for every person, but intimate moments can trigger a crisis for many with autism. As I reviewed my day, I began to see that my son's struggles often led to my own moment of crisis. My son's social anxieties posed problems for both of us, but I was so focused on his issues that I never really dealt with mine. Social anxiety is contagious, so it didn't take long for my own social problems to appear.

My daily inventory was peppered with fear and anger about social interactions. Avoiding meltdowns motivated every decision I made in public, but worries about these episodes often paralyzed me from even venturing out. Controlling my son's environment became my primary purpose in any social situation, and that would often overwhelm me. As time went on, social fatigue became a big source for my moments of crisis, too.

Avoiding a meltdown was the single biggest motivation for any decision I made in public. Seldom was the purpose of our trip successful in those early days. Grocery carts were abandoned. Conversations were abruptly halted. To-do lists went unfulfilled as I tried to avoid those judging stares. Then, when the tantrum finally lost its momentum, I was often left with an emotional hangover that I couldn't shake off. I avoided grocery stores, gas stations, and department stores as long as possible whenever an event embarrassed me enough. When the meltdown inevitably hits, parents are faced with a dilemma: make an escape or ride out the storm.

Of course, my son's meltdowns accelerated so quickly that escape wasn't always an option. Once, I had to wrestle him to the floor in a grocery store, and I struggled to hold him as his tantrum raged on and on and on. When police finally arrived, they found me exhausted by my son's screaming and thrashing. Luckily, policemen were able to keep onlookers at bay, and I was able to tend to my child. Eventually, I was able to calm him, but it was an embarrassing episode to say the least.

As I reviewed those moments of crisis in my life, it came as no surprise that these sorts of incidents always made my list. It wasn't because of any physical security issues. By this point, I was confident and well-practiced with safeholds and de-escalation techniques. These incidents made my list because of those pitying or judging looks from strangers that seemed to haunt me for so long afterward. I had an almost constant worry about what people were thinking, and that self-esteem issue drove me in public situations. This is a common reaction.

Driven by those looks of pity, parents can become so focused on avoiding meltdowns that we develop an uncanny ability to see around corners. We study every room like a grand master of chess, predicting unfolding issues eight steps ahead. Identifying social landmines becomes a superpower, but this strength can easily throw us off balance. Eventually, something makes its way through our defenses, and when a meltdown finally comes, it doesn't take much to tip my scales, either.

When I look back at my moments of crisis, I usually find that my decisions to escape or ride out the storm typically had little to do with my needs or my son's. It wasn't driven by my physical security or my de-escalation routines. If I had time to make a choice, it was usually driven by my audience. More specifically, it was driven by the way I imagined their opinions about me. I would do anything to avoid a judging stare, and my reactions were usually self-centered, manipulative, and controlling.

I've been that parent yelling at a misbehaving child in the grocery store. I have been the baffled father scrambling to master an out-of-control child. There were many times that I've had to scoop up my screaming child and race to my car, careful to avoid eye contact with anyone around me. How sure I was that people were judging me, wondering why my reaction seemed to only make things worse. I was sure that his tantrum reflected on my parenting abilities because I was questioning them myself. Even when someone gave me a pat on the back, I felt I didn't deserve it. I would brush off compliments, sure that what they were really saying was, "What a terrible parent you are. No wonder your child is such a mess." After all, that's what I was thinking. I now know this is common for parents of special needs children. It isn't easy to risk our worst parental moments being played out in front of an audience.

To deal with the spotlight, special needs parents often become award-winning actors on the public stage. When a chaotic meltdown draws stares, we paint on a peaceful expression and attempt to appear unaffected. Onlookers get a gentle smile and a peaceful tone. We ignore questioning looks or requests for help, as we suppress the meltdown with safeholds and complex techniques. A parent might be desperate for that pat on the back but might brush it off entirely when the compliment finally comes. It's one big choreographed dance that has very little to do with actual parenting. It's also a solution that doesn't work. Eventually, when our guard is down or we've had enough, we finally succumb to those hidden emotions ...

A good example of this occurred while I was working as a sports writer for my local newspaper. I attended a lot of high school events, and I often encountered an older woman who always seemed to be there, judging me, when my son suffered a public meltdown. I grew to despise this woman as I painted on a patient face, gathered our belongings, and made my quick escape.

One day, as I scrambled for the door, I caught her staring at us with her typical judgmental look. This was the final straw. I whirled on her and demanded to know what her problem was. Feeling the weight of those looks from the crowd, I retaliated, focusing all of my frustration on this poor, unsuspecting woman.

Instead of fighting back, her face instantly softened. "You are such a good father," she replied. "Is there anything I can do to help?"

The truth is that it is as hard to interpret other people's thoughts as it is for them to interpret mine. For months I had vilified this woman as I confused her admiration for judgment. Every time I was battling my son at a sports contest, I was also battling her. I had projected my own self-esteem issues onto her. It consumed me so much that it distracted me from attending to my son's emotional needs, but this moment of crisis—barking at a stranger while my son needed me the most—was 100 percent in my mind. This particular crisis was self-inflicted. This is just one example of social factors like self-esteem and self-pity conspiring to create a moment of crisis. There were many.

If I wanted to overcome those self-esteem issues that drove me, dominated me, and imprisoned me, I had to abandon my public persona. Once again, the solution was found through sacrifice and service. Professional athletes seldom notice the crowd because they are so focused on the game. We need to do the same. As we shift our focus from ourselves to our children, we can learn to block out the audience, too. Their opinions shouldn't matter, and it really is none of our business. The better we become at focusing on our children's social needs, the easier it is to sacrifice our own.

When we do this, remarkable things happen. First, we learn to block out the audience. Not locked in that emotional turmoil, we begin to make rational decisions based on our experience and our child's needs. We begin to offer solutions, coping strategies, and choices that help our children through their moments of crisis. Less focused on the opinions of others, we begin to build our self-worth with our actions. We begin to learn from our mistakes, so that we can forgive ourselves. We begin to celebrate our successes, even the small ones. Eventually, we start to build a healthy self-esteem, built entirely on our self-evaluation and our estimable actions rather than our perception of other people's opinions. Our self-esteem becomes rooted in fact, not fiction.

Only then are we able to relate properly to the world around us. Parents in crisis often struggle with relationships, but developing a healthy social life is as important for our well-being as clean air, drinkable water, and nourishing food. It's no surprise that social problems dominate our daily lives—and even our dreams—but when we focus too much on this facet of our lives, it always seems to throw us off balance. As we become more weighed down by our child's social delays and communication issues, we become more demanding with our strategies and more conscious of anything posing a threat. Once again, it's like balancing a three-armed scale. The more we focus on social problems, the more we struggle with insecurity or spoiled plans and expectations.

When something threatens our relationships, we retaliate or hold a grudge. We can react more severely when a friend or family member is hurt than when someone hurts us directly. This is even more true when we perceive an injury to our special needs child. Feeling threatened ourselves, we appoint ourselves as defenders not only for ourselves but also for our children, friends, and family. Eventually, we find ourselves in conflict with everyone and everything we encounter. This form of sacrifice—sacrificing our own social needs for our children—is self-defeating. It often gives rise to feelings of guilt, jealousy, and loneliness that lead to more moments of crisis.

We cannot sacrifice our social needs. This is a trap many special needs parents fall into whether they are married or not, but we, too, are social creatures. We cannot sacrifice friendships or romance even though it is easy to justify. Forging deep relationships is one of the biggest challenges for any special needs parent. With so many scheduling challenges, money problems, and responsibilities, it can be difficult to justify social lives. Whether married or single, finding time for romance can seem impossible when juggling complex schedules. With the difficulties and cost of one-on-one, specialized childcare, a night out with friends might seem trivial, but we pay a huge price for sacrificing these pursuits. If we sacrifice them too much, the whole household suffers. Sometimes we need to be creative.

Like our children, we may need accommodations and modifications, but solving this challenge is absolutely necessary for any special needs parent. We cannot ignore this instinctual need because it will not go away. As we ignore our social needs, problems begin to pile up. Eventually, some small inconvenience, some minor disagreement, or some social obstacle will prove to be too much, and we will react instinctively. Oh, that poor person who got in our way. They will feel every frustration, injury, and fear that had been piling up inside of us. Usually, the tipping point comes with someone close to us. Sometimes, it's our children themselves. When social problems build into a crisis, a parent's meltdown usually opens up a gate that isn't easily closed. During times of stress, these social meltdowns can be a regular occurrence, which creates more dysfunction in an already dysfunctional home.

Becoming better aware of ourselves when these social pressures are mounting is crucial if we are going to avoid those bad parenting moments that stem from social triggers. A daily review helps a struggling parent to better understand the conscious and unconscious social issues that plague our daily lives, so that we can prioritize and cope with them before they spark a crisis.

It seems like common sense that a drowning parent can't save a drowning child, but many don't realize they are drowning until it's much too late. My son's struggles with language complicated every aspect of daily living, and that made normal issues loom larger. It wasn't that he didn't have problems with social standing, self-esteem, power dynamics, relationships, and authority; he just lacked the language and coping skills to identify and deal with them, so they often erupted into meltdowns and temper tantrums. His social problems might have looked different, but we both faced the same emotions. In fact, his reactions weren't much different than mine. He reacted in anger when he was hurt, fear when he was threatened, and anxiety when he was confused. So did I.

Once I could learn to identify the social issues in my life and develop healthy coping mechanisms, I was in a better position to be of service to him. If I could remain calm with a sense of distance, I could usually see his confusion, anxiety, or fear register on his face. Since he struggled with language skills, he often couldn't recognize these early emotions in himself. If left to his own devices, those early emotions would fester, grow, and eventually erupt into anger. Sometimes it escalated quickly, sometimes slowly. I began to realize how much we depend on language to solve these emotional problems, and how much his condition complicated his problems. That's where I came in.

By understanding my own emotions and how they erupted into my own moments of crisis, I began to see how social issues were affecting my daily life. As I loosened my grip on the world, I was better able to find peace and purpose. Ironically, the less I tried to avoid meltdowns, the less they occurred. As I became better practiced at handling my own social issues, I developed more patience and tolerance. I became part of my son's solution rather than one more problem he had to overcome, and we were finally able to swim to safety.

Once I began to see the crisis in me, it became easier to spot them in my child. As I began to understand how my crisis builds and how it manifests in me, it became easier to relate to my son's daily outbreaks. I began to see how his own plans and expectations would get threatened, and I could almost predict the outbreak. I could begin to understand his insecurities or social obstacles and how they manifested in him. Armed with an understanding of his state of mind, I could begin to work with him. I could use my own experience to help give voice to his problems.

In order to share my experiences, I have to understand them myself. When dealing with my insecurities, it was useful to talk about them with somebody who would understand. We can use the same approach that we used with insecurities. Many of us will find that we've never had a frank discussion about self-esteem issues or communication problems, so it might take some practice. The effort will be worth it as we gain perspective on ourselves, along with coping strategies and solutions. The more at ease we become with these uncomfortable conversations, the better prepared we will be to discuss these issues with our children.

Then, it takes action. Sure, we may have to abandon half-filled shopping carts if social anxiety becomes too much for our children, but it's an opportunity to talk to them about how we overcome these same emotions in our lives. Before heading out, we can have proactive discussions with our children, explaining the purpose of our trip, discussing expectations and coping strategies. During the excursion, we can continue the discussion, watching for feedback or signs of stress. We can be flexible with our plans, remembering to be hard on ourselves but gentle on our children. It helps if we can simplify our trips. It is often easier to make multiple short trips than one long outing. At the first sign of struggle, we should find a place that's quiet and secure. Then, we can talk about it before it builds into a crisis for them. Finding a solution to social problems is something that a parent and child can do together.

Once the parent has gained confidence, this becomes easier. Once we begin to chip away at our own social issues, we are better able to offer solutions that work to our children. During this process, the parent becomes a better mentor, a confident partner, and a source of strength and support. When we do it well, we're able to concentrate on our children's issues more than our own. We stop trying to manage triggers, and we begin to mentor solutions. The more we focus on our children, the less we will focus on those onlookers. We become more like the athlete, so engrossed in the game that we become unaware of the crowd. We begin to develop an emotional distance, create ideals, and work toward them.

This emotional distance has other benefits as well. When I'm not in self-defense mode, I can see the looks of others as an opportunity instead of a slight. When I look back on that incident in my courtyard, I was too involved to do any good for my son or those boys. That's the way it always was during those public meltdowns where I was trying to avoid glances. I repeatedly missed opportunities for support and education. My lack of distance from my son's crisis affected my thinking and my actions, so I missed opportunities to help anyone, even myself.

Social issues are unavoidable. Everyone has them whether they have special needs or not. By becoming adept at recognizing, discussing, and resolving these issues within ourselves, we help develop one more parenting tool in our arsenal. Left unchecked, social issues throw us off balance. They increase any existing security issues. They complicate our plans and routines.

Solving social issues opens up the world to us and our children.

# CHAPTER SIX
*The Scorecard: Plans, Expectations, and Routines*

Today's society celebrates success. At times, it seems as if everybody is championing some sort of achievement, but in a special needs home, there is nothing that feels more out of reach. Success feels impossible when our daily lives are filled with the constant struggle just to keep our heads above water. So often, special needs parents are forced to put their own plans and expectations on hold as they struggle to balance doctor's visits, childcare, and daily responsibilities. Even the most mundane daily tasks require more time, effort, and planning when accommodating a child's special needs into the schedule. Financial and emotional security is often sacrificed for flexibility. Chasing a pat on the back at work or a meaningful place in society seems selfish in light of a child's special needs, so these very things that are taken for granted by most people can feel out of reach to special needs parents and their families.

    So many moments of crisis can be traced back to the daily obstacles that hinder our success. Plans go unfinished. Expectations have to be constantly shifted and lowered. Successfully checking off an item on our to-do lists often requires complex planning and work-arounds. Looking at the day ahead of us, it's easy to fall into pessimism, recognizing that something unexpected is likely to come up and disrupt our carefully planned system. Daily routines are often upended by meltdowns or tantrums. Even if we are successful, our celebration is often clouded by the realization that it took longer than expected. Schedules and routines can never be written in ink because everything is always subject to change. We begin to expect delays and obstacles, and we become willing to do whatever it takes to avoid failure and frustration.

    Human beings are creatures of habit. Most of us thrive on routines, but this presents an incredible challenge in special needs homes. Long before my son's condition was diagnosed, specialists stressed that routines would be helpful. It's the one point that behavioral experts can agree upon. Routines and schedules are extremely helpful for autistic children since they are already subject to repetitive patterns of behavior, and my son was no exception. Right from the start, he was extraordinarily disciplined when it came to certain routines, like sleep schedules and meal plans. Everything from entertainment to bathroom breaks needed to fit perfectly into his daily program. It helped that his school day was well structured. His daily routines were precise, so creating a stable and comfortable environment became the main goal in our household. At first, it seemed like the solution we craved.

From the moment my son entered preschool, we learned a lot from his teachers about implementing structure and routine throughout his day. Specialists stressed the importance of consistency, and that seemed to work wonders in our home. The more we structured our family's daily activities, the less stress my son seemed to exhibit. There was even a slight decrease in his daily meltdowns and tantrums when a strict plan was implemented in our home. We embraced this new order. Every room in our apartment had a calendar and a clock, and my son responded right away. When he learned to write, he began to craft detailed lists of people, activities, and events. He began to schedule visits with family and friends, and this was a welcomed change to his behavior. He paid special attention to birthdays, anniversaries, holidays, and regularly scheduled events. The more disciplined we were in the home, the less stressed he seemed to be ... at first.

Of course, parents quickly realize that an overly disciplined routine creates its own challenges. What happens when the routines, themselves, become our biggest obstacle? As our lives became more structured, my son began to get anxious when schedules weren't met or changes were introduced. After a while, any change to his expectations could spark a tantrum. So many of

## THE SCORECARD

my son's moments of crisis were sparked by interruptions to a schedule he created, and they still are. As we became more disciplined in our lives, it almost seemed to reinforce the demands he would make on the world around him. Consequently, anything that upset his routines would create stress for both of us. Anything that wasn't proactively scheduled in our daily plan could spark a crisis in him—or me.

The more we scheduled our day, the less flexible we both became. If something was late, it would add to our stress. If something was interrupted, it could spark a moment of panic, so I began to throw more effort into controlling our schedules and our environment. This is a fairly common reaction when a parent is blindly driven to avoid anything that might spoil a plan and upset their child. Trying to get our way becomes an art form, pitting us in direct conflict with every obstacle in our path. We may act friendly and calm to achieve our goal, but we can just as easily come across as ruthlessly demanding. Unfortunately, the more we try to get our way, the more out of control everything seems to be. Over time, those very schedules, designed to bring peace and order into our lives, become a big source of stress and chaos. In this way, our solution can actually become our biggest problem.

In the classroom, routines are easier to enact because the environment is easier to control. It has to be since routines are dictated by lesson plans, curriculum, and the time frames of a school day. Success and failure are easily measured when a school bell rings, but that doesn't play out as smoothly in the real world when goals aren't as concrete or measurable. When the child and the parent return home, tired after a busy day, it can often be hard to stay on task. After all, what is the task? Often there are conflicting priorities, such as making dinner, other household chores, and the competing needs of other household members.

It's not always possible to provide the same level of one-on-one focus as in a school setting. There isn't a team of specialists at hand when a meltdown occurs, and there's no school bell to signal a new task or school bus to offer relief at the end of our day.

Every day there are a number of unexpected changes to any routine, but these could quickly escalate into moments of crisis in our home. Distractions and special events upended the schedule, and my son would melt down. An unscheduled event in the middle of the week could upset the whole balance of our day. An unavoidable change to the weekend routine could create an emotional crisis for my son. Every time these sorts of events would come up, it would require extra planning, including setting expectations and scripting behavior or conversations.

Frustration and anxiety grew as checking off items on our list became the ultimate goal. There was always a worry that something wouldn't go as planned. Sometimes, if an event was too big or too inconvenient, it might be easier to skip it entirely than to take on the extra preparation required. In this way, strict routines and overly scheduled activities lead to even more isolation and insecurity for the special needs family. If we too strictly adhere to our schedules, the schedules themselves become a problem. Homes become prisons with parents as the wardens. The children, trapped in the very routines that are designed for comfort and stability, often revolt.

My son's issues were compounded by his condition. As a child, he was diagnosed as a calendar savant. It seemed like a superpower at first. Given an important date like a birthday or anniversary, he'd instantly calculate the day of the week in his head. If prompted about a particular day in the past, he could recall very specific details like weather, activities, and people he encountered. He was also fixated on future schedules. He would circle vacation dates on the calendar years in advance. He could predict future weekends with either parent, so that visitation schedules were set in stone. He could calculate dates for shifting holidays like Mother's Day or Easter so easily that it became a game for us, and it proved to be an amazing performance that would dazzle friends and family. My son would often talk about future events for months—or even years—in advance. For someone who struggled with opening conversations, he quickly realized that asking someone their birthday (and instantly calculating the day of the week that it happened) was a great way to connect with strangers and friends. His skills are incredible, and his reputation for dates and calendars is legendary.

But there was another side to this gift. If my son added an

event to his mind's calendar, it was carved in stone. Plans were more like demands, and any variation might trigger a tantrum. As the day arrived, he would become more obsessed with his plans. Sometimes, he would relive specific days, months, and years when the calendars lined up with past events. If there were traumatic events, difficult dates, deaths, or fears from one year that fell on the same day of the week in the current year, he relived the day and all the emotions associated with it. Sure, ours was an extreme example of routines paralyzing a child, but it is common for all children to have additional stress when routines are disrupted.

When we place too much importance on plans and expectations, it isn't hard to lose perspective. During daily reviews, it becomes easy to see how often our goals, expectations, routines, schedules, and ambitions drive us throughout our day, and we begin to see how much emotional turmoil stems from not getting our way. We usually find that obstacles to our success can trigger a moment of crisis more than any other cause. A perfect example in my life was that youth baseball tournament, and the crisis that unfolded when my plans began to unravel.

My overly ambitious schedule at the tournament was carefully designed to balance my parenting duties and my work responsibilities, but my plan quickly broke down because of factors outside of my control. To avoid the chaos of a meltdown, I left early. But that didn't solve the problem. The more I focused on controlling my son's behavior, the more it put us at odds with one

## THE SCORECARD

another. The more I fought to get my way, the more the situation devolved. My son's crisis was sparked early in our battle, but my crisis developed over time as I fought to regain control of the situation. Eventually, it drove me to the most selfish action that a parent can do. I was demanding, selfish, unloving, and emotionally unavailable at the very moment that he needed a parent the most.

This wasn't an isolated event. My early inventories were littered with moments of crisis that erupted when my plans unraveled. With each example, I saw that I became more and more demanding as the obstacles piled up in my way. At times, there were wars raging inside of me as I tried to control my son, my environment, and anyone we encountered. The more I tried to fight for balance and order, the more it seemed to elude us. The more I tried to avoid my son's chaotic meltdowns, the more they seemed to happen, affecting both him and me. As we exert increasing pressure on those around us, especially our special needs children, they begin to revolt until the very structure that was designed to produce order and balance brings about moments of disorder and chaos.

On most days, I was able to provide him with the compassion and love that he needed even if it was through gritted teeth. I was committed to helping him silence his rage, and most days comforting him was my main goal. I pledged to give him affection, and I often succeeded. I vowed to have patience and tolerance when he struggled, and I usually lived up to that promise.

But on many days, I fell short. I found that I was often unable to offer peace and comfort, because you can't give something away if you don't have it to give. We were both struggling with the same things at the same time, but we weren't working through it together. In fact, we were competing in a sick battle over our plans and expectations, although I didn't realize it at the time. This happened more times than I'd like to admit.

Obstacles to my plans and expectations became a problem very early in my parenting career because there are very few things that shatter a parent's plans and expectations more than a child's special needs diagnosis. When the specialist told me that my son's life wouldn't be normal, it was as if a door was suddenly slammed on both of our lives. My past hardly prepared me for the sure struggles that I perceived ahead of us. My present life was already full of chaos and uncertainty, but now all my future goals, expectations, and ambitions were thrown out the window. In that instant that the diagnosis was cemented, it snuffed out any lingering hope that life would return to "normal" for me or for my son. The sense of order, balance, and fairness was crushed by a very real panic about the future.

All these issues were compounded by concerns about my son's future. How would he find purpose? How would his ambitions be met? How would he find success, love, and friendship? Could he ever be self-sufficient? Would he be safe and protected? Would he find happiness?

## THE SCORECARD

A flood of fears consumed me when his condition finally earned a name. We had traveled to the state capital to have him seen by a world expert at a prominent children's hospital. The diagnosis was delivered, and it sent my thoughts spiraling over money and security issues, fears about his and my relationships, along with a flurry of other unforeseen obstacles and barriers. In that instant, I realized that my whole life plan had to be abandoned, and another one had to be developed quickly. This brought a sense of panic and impending doom. How can life have order and meaning? There was certainly nothing fair about my son's condition. I barely heard anything else that the doctor told me after the diagnosis. The drive home was lonely and scary.

Everybody, certainly every parent, has to face obstacles to the plans we create for our children, but nobody has to face as many obstacles or as many unknowns as a parent of a special needs child. Long before my son's diagnosis was confirmed, our lives were spinning out of control. His disruptive behavioral issues and regular meltdowns were already impacting our daily schedules and routines. Simple tasks required extra effort and planning. Everyday living was constantly threatened by obstacles to our schedules and routines. My long-term plans and ambitions were already thrown out the window long before the diagnosis confirmed my fears. The strain that this put on my home life, my work life, and my relationships was already thrusting me to the brink of crisis. Our peaceful home had become a battlefield.

We weren't unique. In one way or another, obstacles to daily living become the central theme in the lives of all special needs children and their families. These unique threats creep into our ordinary thoughts, adding to those typical, everyday stressors that everyone encounters in the course of daily living. It isn't hard to see how our ambitions become so easily warped. Compounded by my fears of the future, everything seemed to loom larger than life. I began to put more effort into my parenting and felt more emotional at every setback. Armed with the conviction that my son's threatened future was unfair, I threw myself even harder into protecting him. Problems piled up and often led to crisis—for him and for me. It was as if everyone and everything was pressing my buttons, and it was only a matter of time until someone pressed the wrong one.

I was acutely aware of any of my plans that failed, and I became angry and jealous whenever I noticed other people's success. After a while, I began to keep score with a running tally in my head. I was locked in a competition with everyone around me, but they had no idea about my scorecard. Over time, I became more desperate for wins and more critical about other people's victories. I began to see everyone around me as an opponent, and I seemed to be losing every contest. It made perfect sense to me when I overreacted to some small conflict or disagreement. I felt justified by my self-pity and fueled by my losing score. Whenever we keep score, we are bound to lose. It's hard to be honest and

## THE SCORECARD

straightforward, loving and self-sacrificing, when we are deadlocked in a sick competition ... and losing.

All around me, people were pressing my buttons without knowing it. A person in the grocery store blocking the aisle when my son was beginning to fidget could prove to be one obstacle too many. Two people talking in front of the item I needed to purchase might be the last straw if they ignored my silent pleas to move out of my way. The tipping point could be something as simple as a person ahead of me in line taking too much time to unload their cart. When we are looking for these sorts of obstacles, it isn't hard to find them.

There comes a point when people don't even have to come into direct contact with us to push our buttons. Jealousy might get sparked by another shopper navigating a store effortlessly while we're struggling. It is surprising how much a parent in crisis can be angered when someone gets in our way, but it is harder to explain how someone else's success can anger us—even if it has nothing to do with our success or failure. We can be just easily annoyed by the person in the next checkout line who rings out quicker than us or a well-behaved child when ours is fussing. At times, it can feel as if everyone else is taunting us, challenging us, or beating us at a game they didn't even know they were playing.

Of course, my son was best at pressing my buttons. He had done it so often and for so long that I was in constant fear and dread that it would happen again. I developed complex schemes and detailed plans to try to avoid his behavioral issues. But even if they were initially successful, those schemes would eventually fail. So I'd try harder the next time only to have it upended by something else unexpected.

What was going to set off my child? This almost became an obsession for me. Out of sheer necessity, I became good at spotting problems before they happened like a lifeguard on a crowded beach. One mistake on my part could lead to hours of meltdown, so I could be quite demanding that people follow my plans. After a while, it seemed that everybody was consciously working against me. The more I tried to head off problems, the more people seemed to upend my plan. It was almost as if they were doing it on purpose, and my losses were piling up.

It is impossible to account for all the unpredictable hurdles in a special needs household, so parents begin to develop elaborate schemes for avoiding problems. Over time, we can develop a detailed script in our heads, and we get frustrated when people don't follow the lines we've written. The more we try to force our script on the world around us, the more we begin to notice how others don't act the way they should. In this state of mind, the score never seems to work out in our favor. The more we focus on wins and losses, the more we double down on our script. We quickly fall out of balance.

The more we focus on success, the more we notice our insecurities. The more we compete with the people around us—

even our special needs child—the more we struggle with relationships. Competition over plans, expectations, and routines makes intimacy, patience, and forgiveness impossible. We soon find ourselves in conflict with anybody who gets in the way of our plans and schedules. We can even act out against our rivals before they strike, and it's easy to justify any bad behavior with the scorecards we keep.

Pity the person who finally tips the scales. It doesn't matter whether it's on purpose or by accident. Get in our way at the wrong time, and it could prove disastrous. Even a small slight could prove to be the final straw. Once that moment of crisis is reached, it opens the floodgates. Out comes a pent-up wave of venom. On the other hand, if failures continue to pile up on our tallies, we may choose to give up entirely. Nobody reacts well in a crisis.

The tipping point for so many moments of crisis can be easily traced back to a moment of competing priorities. Those detailed plans and schedules carefully crafted to bring about balance and order can suddenly transform into the very cause of our conflicts. Fighting to stay on schedule can put us in direct competition with the very success that we're trying to achieve. When reviewing those conflicts between parent and child or between any two household members, plans and expectations are often at the center of the crisis.

As I continue to review those moments of crisis, I finally begin to understand how my ambitions collide with my son's and everybody else's. I begin to see that he reacts much like me when his schedule is threatened. Those side trips to the store, the normal interruptions that we face during the day, and the special events like birthday parties, holidays, and family events create an obstacle for both of us.

With good intentions I get bogged down in preparations and fixes, while he struggles with changes to his patterns. I make demands to try to keep order. He fights to hold on to his routine, and it puts us both in a position where we fight to get our way. We are both so rigid in our plans that any threat to our routines forms the first link in a chain of events that leads to a meltdown. Although I couldn't see it before my daily inventory, I soon began to see that people often find themselves in opposing positions due to conflicting plans and priorities. Each individual fights to get their way and neither succeeds when the competition boils over.

So, what can we do about it? How do we find balance between our plans and the realities of life? If we are convinced that we cannot change the world around us or force people to follow our scripts, then our only choice is to flip the script. We need to be easier on others, recognizing their good intentions rather than focusing solely on the actions that may get in our way. And we need to be harder on ourselves rather than focusing on our intentions and the unreasonable demands we make on everyone else. We have to set a better, more realistic ideal when it comes to our plans and expectations.

## THE SCORECARD

Once again, sacrifice and service are the answer.

It is clear that my actions fell short of my ideals, especially with my son, so I had to redefine my goals. At times, I had to lower expectations, and I definitely had to find a better outlet than sheer determination when something threatened my plans. The best way to do that, I've found, is to redirect my thinking. Rather than trying to force my plans onto a situation, I had to embrace those obstacles as my ultimate plan. I had to see them as opportunities for parenting service. To overcome obstacles to my plans and expectations, I had to find a way to lessen my expectations.

My son, himself, was the answer. It was easy to see that I struggled with disruptions, but it was just as easy to see that he struggled more. As I became more aware of those threats to my routines, I began to gain a better understanding of the way he struggled with threats to his routines. Instead of working so hard to avoid obstacles to my plan, I had to find a way to embrace those obstacles. Instead of trying to navigate around those obstacles so that I could enjoy my life, I had to realize that those obstacles were my life. By learning to embrace interruptions and failed plans, I could finally offer my son a solution when something inevitably spoiled his expectations. If I could sacrifice my unreasonable expectations for fairness and success, I could focus on mentoring my son through the emotional minefield of unfair situations and upended schedules.

When I successfully adopt this attitude, I am finally able to stop focusing on problems. Instead, I learn how to live with interruptions and disappointments. Once our plans and expectations become right-sized, we finally begin to find balance in our lives. As we become less competitive, we become more secure. As the number of conflicts subside, our social issues lessen. When we are properly balanced, it becomes more difficult to be thrown into crisis. Our relationships improve. We find it easier to be honest and straightforward with others, and we are more successful at being unselfish and loving.

Embracing change with my son became a game that we could win together. He was never interested in board games or typical play, but we learned to play together throughout our day, rolling with the punches, and dealing with disappointment. Sometimes, we can even laugh at ourselves when we make mistakes. Struggling to make sense of the world around him continues to be my son's biggest challenge, but he has become less anxious in public settings over the years because we have become more comfortable with things not going our way. We have had far more successes than failures as we've become less competitive with each other and the world around us. This has led to many truly intimate moments and serendipitous encounters.

Perfection is no longer the expectation, but my daily review continues to uncover moments where things didn't work out as I expected. At times, I still find myself competing with others, keeping score, and forcing the script in my head, but these

## THE SCORECARD

moments rarely erupt in temper tantrums or meltdowns anymore. Instead, my daily review serves as a sort of report card on my progress, and steady improvement has become the reasonable expectation. It is easier to focus on other people and situations when things don't go as planned, but my daily review forces me to look at myself. Like most people, my emotions spike when some person or situation gets in the way of my goals, but now I'm able to look at the plans themselves. I can finally see how unreasonable demands can set me up for failure, and I can usually keep myself from retaliating when I see how my expectations played a role in a disagreement.

There's another advantage to tracking my progress and understanding how I'm affected by spoiled plans and expectations. For so long it was impossible to discuss my daily struggles with others—even specialists—because most people can't identify with the unique obstacles we face as special needs parents. Consequently, they were rarely in a position to offer reasonable advice or understanding. How could they? But all people deal with failed expectations, unreasonable expectations, and unforeseen obstacles. When approached about the feelings associated with failure rather than the specifics about the failures themselves, people are usually happy to share similar experiences from their lives. More importantly, they can share their solutions, allowing us to develop better coping mechanisms when situations don't go as planned. These conversations will better prepare us to mentor our children when they encounter their own struggles with plans and expectations.

When getting our way is the ultimate goal, there can be no peace. When peace is the ultimate goal, we cannot focus so much on getting our way. For any parent in crisis, peace of mind seems impossible because navigating a daily schedule can feel like a dangerous tightrope walk. Most decisions feel like a bad choice between two lesser evils, and every wrong answer could signal the next crisis for us or our children. It's a wrestling match that nobody seems to win. But if we adopt a different approach, embrace those obstacles in our path, and learn to enjoy the ride, we can find peace and a purpose.

Life can be about the journey, not the destination. That's a game that everybody can win.

# CHAPTER SEVEN

*Dysfunction Junction: Divorce and Separation*

---

Even when everything is going well in a relationship, co-parenting may be one of the most difficult endeavors for any two people. It takes a level of commitment and cooperation unlike anything else. To be successful, people have to put aside their individual ambitions, insecurities, and social needs in order to cooperate toward a shared objective. The process goes on for decades, and experience is hammered out over time through trial and error. Opportunities for conflict abound as a family's limited resources are taxed with innumerable mental and physical obstacles affecting time, money, ambitions, relationships and power dynamics. At every turn, with every decision, after every problem, demands increase that can escalate an individual, a couple, or the whole family into crisis. There is nothing more vulnerable than the family unit.

The cost of raising a family can affect every household at every social level. As the family grows, housing becomes more expensive. The household budget will need to be stretched to meet the need for additional food, clothing, health care, and childcare. At every stage of development, there are new worries about security, from education and transportation costs to social expenses and leisure activities.

Of course, finances aren't the only challenges faced by parents. Balancing family and work life creates obstacles with every additional schedule and routine. Expectations shift at every new stage with setbacks possible at every turn. As the child's social circle widens, it creates new challenges with each new friend or activity. Family life brings many joys and challenges, but each change can contribute to increased stress. When something has to give, too many times it's the marriage itself. Arguments, dysfunction, and divorce can contribute to additional problems for family function.

When the family includes a child with special needs, those typical family stressors can multiply exponentially. There have been a number of marriage studies conducted since the 1980s. Some have looked at families dealing with chronic stress and major depression. Others have focused on the impact of general disabilities, and most recently a handful of studies focused on the effect of autism spectrum disorder on the family unit. Most have shown a measurable increase in dysfunction, separation, and divorce rates. Some studies have suggested divorce rates as much as

80 percent higher than average when a child is suffering from disability. Even if families manage to avoid separation or divorce, these homes are often strained in ways that ordinary families cannot understand.

For the special needs parents, these studies merely demonstrate what we already know: Raising a special needs child can add stress to every person in the household. Many families succumb to these pressures, and this presents an even bigger challenge to daily living. How can a family, already stressed to the breaking point, continue to cooperate at the level needed to raise a special needs child? Can a family recover emotionally? Can they cooperate despite their differences? Can they survive or even thrive as a family once a romantic relationship has come to an end? Fortunately, the answer to all these questions is a resounding "Yes!"

Make no mistake, navigating divorce, separation or dysfunction is no easy task. When one struggling household is suddenly divided into two, it magnifies an already confusing situation. Suddenly, there are additional challenges with schedules, child custody issues, visitation constraints, and child support demands. These challenges must be ironed out at the same time that living expenses increase as individuals scramble to support multiple households. Each one of these obstacles is made more difficult by two parents struggling with an open emotional wound. It is hard enough for clashing parents to develop coping mechanisms for themselves, but a child with special needs might not have the most basic coping skills necessary to navigate such an emotional roller coaster.

Routines are thrown out the window. Financial challenges and time management stresses are suddenly multiplied, and already isolated parents can get bogged down in bitterness, resentment, guilt, jealousy, grief, and loneliness. A family that is already in turmoil can suddenly find itself in crisis—separately as individuals or together as a group.

All families are taxed by security issues, packed schedules, and social challenges, but a child with special needs takes that stress to a different level. Food and social constraints, additional health-care costs, along with the need for specialized, individual childcare adds to the expenses of normal daily living. Dealing with the medical, social, and routine challenges of a special needs child can impact both parents' earning potential, and that can compound an already difficult situation. If there are multiple children, those normal sibling rivalry issues are made worse as one child's needs get sidelined by the needs of another. Whether the threat is actual or perceived doesn't seem to matter.

With lifelong worries about safety and insecurities, along with added health-care needs, childcare costs, and a host of other issues that make these families more vulnerable, it is easy to see why a special needs family faces more stress and uncertainty than families without a special needs child. The demands of a special needs child can be overwhelming to both one- and two-parent households, even if one parent is able to stay home to care for the child. But when single parents find themselves forced to balance the responsibilities of home and work with the needs of a special child and the demands of a difficult co-parenting situation, life can often feel hopeless. Add any underemployment or unemployment issue to the very real poverty issues already faced by special needs homes, and every day can result in a crisis—and it often does.

There is no easy way to say it. Divorce and separation are difficult. Although some people handle it better than others, all divorced parents must learn to deal with anger and resentment about past injuries, the competition of co-parenting within two separate households, and a whole host of additional worries and uncertainties about the future.

Most of all, divorce is difficult for the children. Caught between two warring parents, any child can flounder. But with a special needs child, divorce can be the final straw. There are hundreds of books written about the challenges children face in divorced households, but when there's a special needs child involved, those challenges loom larger and overcoming them quickly is even more important. With communication and intimacy problems coming to a head in the family, progress can be stunted for these special needs children who are already struggling with the obstacles of the real world.

For an autistic child, intimacy is already a big problem, so when parents struggle with intimacy issues, the impact on these children can be even greater. My son's meltdowns increased during my divorce even though we worked hard to shield him from negativity. There can be no intimacy when parents are competing for time, money, and love. So as parents struggle, children struggle, and problems mount. Honest communication becomes more difficult. Any attempt at self-sacrificing can stop. Dysfunction and bitterness might replace love and caring. Locked in this state, parents and children often retreat into self-defense modes where cooperation becomes impossible.

Perhaps you and your co-parent went through a good breakup. Perhaps there weren't a lot of hard feelings or lingering injuries between you. Of course, that's ideal. But even in this situation there are challenges with the new living arrangement that still need to be addressed. Even when a family manages to stay together, these same stressors can bring a high level of dysfunction into the household.

Just to be clear, this is not a book about liking your ex. There is no magic wand, except forgiveness, for getting along or for being friendly. Finding peace and satisfaction takes time and effort on both sides, and that isn't always something that both parents can commit to embracing. The good news is that it's not necessary to be on the same page—or even to like each other—to form an ideal co-parenting dynamic. Once that beginning is made, it can prove to be a foundation for a loving, intimate co-parenting situation regardless of your feelings for one another.

So, how is that possible? I found that partnership with my ex was the biggest challenge I faced in parenting a special needs child. I came from a family that didn't get divorced. In my immediate family, I was the only one. Even with my extended family, there were very few divorces or separations. So when my marriage came to an end, I found myself poorly equipped to handle its effects, and I had no family members experienced enough to help me. Most of my worst behavior can be traced back to those turbulent years, but I found some principles that helped to guide me through and eventually overcome it.

The most important principle for successful co-parenting is unity. A child's confidence and security depend on the strength of the family unit. Without a stable environment every child struggles, but for a special needs child, struggling to make sense of the world around them, a stable home is more valuable than gold. So unifying a family must be the primary goal.

This immediately poses some big obstacles. How does one cooperate with an "ex?" How do two people disregard past hurts to come together as a team? How does a person lower his or her guard to allow an ex back into their life on a daily basis? How does somebody lay aside competition with an ex and begin to sacrifice their own needs for the good of the group? These challenges are impossible without a change in perspective. A good place to begin is the language of breaking up.

Nobody can build a relationship with an ex. An "ex," by

any definition, means that there is no relationship to build. I often found that my perspective was skewed by my own ill feelings. I had trouble being totally open and honest when I was trying to protect myself. It was just as hard to be self-sacrificing or straightforward with my ex during those early days of our breakup. To be loving was out of the question. Co-parenting under these conditions proved to be impossible.

Of course, this attitude only served to complicate our family dynamics, and our son was trapped in the middle. Those transitions from one household to the other were fraught with difficulties, arguments, and snubs. Transitions are difficult for any child, but for my special needs child these were his most difficult times. He already struggled with transitions from school to home or between events and activities, but these transitions between homes were aggravated by two exes struggling with resentment and hurt. I began to blame my ex for my son's behavioral issues, my personal problems, and the moments of crisis that flared up during these transitions. Eventually, even my closest friends began to tire of my frequent rants about my ex.

I eventually realized that it was nearly impossible to build a relationship with an ex because there's no foundation left to build upon. There's no ideal to strive toward. The starting point for any "ex" relationship is the ending point of another, failed relationship. To love, honor and cherish an ex is virtually impossible. To call someone an ex is like labeling another unavoidable failure. Once the romantic relationship has ended, there's nothing to rebuild. That's not to say that reconciliation is impossible—or even undesirable. But for most people at the end of a relationship, the "ex" label is just another barrier that is unhelpful when trying to build trust, love, or partnership.

On the other hand, my divorce signaled the end of only one relationship. There was still another, more important relationship that desperately needed to be salvaged. That was the relationship with my child's mother. She was my partner in the only business that really mattered—raising our special needs son. It became apparent early on that this was the relationship that I needed to focus on more than anything else. That all starts with the name.

Calling my son's mother "Jack's mother" was a turning point for me. Even with hurt feelings and pride continuing to block any real intimate partnership with my ex, I still found that I could love my son's mother—even if it was begrudgingly. I found that I could be selfless and sacrificing for my son's mother, even if I still harbored resentment toward my "ex." It is impossible to have an intimate relationship if we are bogged down in competition and rivalries, but I found that it was harder to compete with my son's mother than with my ex. Even though I struggled to love my ex-wife, it was easier to love, honor, and cherish my son's mother. I can still remember the day that I committed to calling her "Jack's mother." I'm not sure if it was a turning point in her healing, but it was definitely a turning point in mine.

Until this point, it was easy to trace each emotional crisis back to my ex. My anger provided me with excuses for everything that was wrong with my life. During my seemingly daily moment of crisis, I could see her words and actions as the cause of all my problems. But afterward, when I sat down and evaluated what was going on inside of me during those moments of crisis, I could see that it wasn't that she pressed my buttons. It was the buttons themselves—demands on her, my son, and me that were caused by my routines, my expectations, my security, and my relationships. In other words, those moments of crisis with my son's mother were no different than any other crisis in my life. They had the same causes, and those causes were inside me.

It was easy to justify any demands I made on my ex, but I began to see that it wasn't as easy to place unreasonable demands on my son's mother. Who was I to demand that she act a certain way, put my needs first, or consider me when having a relationship with her son? It seemed almost ridiculous that these things mattered so much to me. After all, my needs aren't important in a parenting situation. My son's needs were all that mattered. Rather than focusing on me and my needs, I began to focus on helping my son and his mother. Rather than fighting to get my way, I began to focus on getting out of their way. With practice, I found that there were fewer sparks to flare into conflicts when I remained focused on my son and when I thought of my ex as "Jack's mother." I finally realized that my emotions had more to do with the demands I was imposing in my head than anything that anyone else was saying or doing. At the very least, my demands—not their words or actions—were the only things I had any real control over, and I was doing a poor job at it.

It wasn't an overnight matter, but that commitment to love my son's mother rather than compete with my "ex" proved to be one of the best decisions I've ever made. The proof came many years later after a meeting with my son's teacher, the school specialists, and the board of education. At the end of the meeting, one of them mentioned my "wife."

I quickly corrected her. (During my review of that day, this moment proved to be the closest I came to a moment of crisis that day because it caught me off guard. My reaction to this innocent mention of a spouse was met by an instinctual emotional response. I got defensive). "We're no longer married," I said.

"Really?" she asked. Her face registered actual surprise. "I thought you were a couple."

Of course, this was after many years of healing and practice by both of us, but it was proof that we had built a harmonious family. Someone who worked with my child every day had mistaken two non-romantic co-parents as a happy, loving couple, which in fact we had truly become. It turned out to be one of the best compliments I've ever received for my parenting.

Today I can happily say that I love my son's mother

completely, and I think she would probably say the same. It's not romantic love, but it's one of our family's best achievements. Our son has two loving parents. Sure, we disagree. Sure, we sometimes have our difficulties, but that is true of any couple—married or not. The one thing I'm sure of is that there is only one person who loves and cares for my son as much as me, and that is my son's mother. It is so much better to be co-parents rather than to be rivals.

The real question is, how do I get to a point where I can love a co-parent rather than compete with them? For me, it took a conscious effort, a lot of self-inventory, and too many mistakes to count. The whole process started by calling her "Jack's mom" instead of "my ex." Only then was I able to start rebuilding the love that is so necessary in a family unit. Only then was I able to stop focusing on past hurts and threats to my self-esteem and expectations. I have yet to find a shortcut. It can be a very long period of rebuilding, but it's a much healthier commitment than the alternative.

As soon as I became committed to teamwork, I was finally able to tackle all of the dysfunctional issues that needed to be corrected. Once I was able to see my son's mother as an equal member of the parenting team, I was ready to face issues with power dynamics and authority, differences in parenting styles, inequalities, and disagreements. Once I had embraced my role as a co-parent, I was better able to be open-minded, patient, and tolerant. I soon realized that the more I focused on fixing myself, the less I felt the need to fix others. Family harmony began to win over any competition.

Power dynamics are often the biggest issue between households during this process of healing, and if it's not solved the problem can go on indefinitely. Forming a healthy team is impossible unless all team members are allowed to contribute, participate in the decision-making, and dispute any past decision that might not be working to everyone's satisfaction. Individual needs must take a back seat to the needs of the group, and that is not easy when relationships are clouded by emotions and power struggles. Unless there's a danger to the child, everyone has to be a welcome member and an equal participant.

Oftentimes, the courts are involved. Whether it's an agreement before a judge, a custody hearing, or a mediation, the ultimate goal is to establish a working parenting plan. Coming up with a fair plan can be hard, but it's the first, necessary step. Once an ideal is established, both parties can begin to work toward it.

Drafting a fair custody agreement can feel like an impossible task, and it can spark all sorts of emotional crises while it's being ironed out. Then, it can spark even more crises when it's wielded as a weapon by one parent or another every time a dispute comes up. These agreements, by their very nature, seem to work against the goal of family unity. What parent wants to be separated from their child for days or hours at a time? What parent wants to lose access to their child or miss important milestones? Who can really schedule a relationship when life is so unpredictable? Who wants to draft boundaries when love is supposed to be unconditional? The best agreements are reached when viewed as a parenting plan between co-parents rather than a war treaty drawn between winners and losers. Cooperation should be the goal, and agreements are always subject to change as needs within the family change. Flexibility and open-mindedness are key.

Often, the process requires lawyers and mediators, but not always. If emotions can be put aside, and an honest conversation can be had, an agreement can be accomplished without a judge's ruling. The most important thing is what's best for the child, not the parent. Is shared custody best or is that too much back-and-forth for a special needs child? Are there other options? Negotiation and compromise are the most important components of any successful agreement.

Of course, divorce isn't the only way that co-parenting dynamics can be challenged. It might be that parents were never married. It might be that the relationship was never equal in time or cost. It might be that a goal of fifty-fifty isn't possible or even ideal. Whatever your situation turns out to be, it's the access to a relationship with the child that should always be equal. Unless a relationship is harmful to the welfare of the child, co-parenting should never be about excluding or limiting a child's access to a loving parent. The same can be said about stepparents, romantic partners, and friends of either parent. The more people who love a child, the better, especially when the child has special needs. Even if that means that one or both parents will feel threatened or hurt, the child's needs must come first. That is only possible if family unity is the ultimate goal.

Discussing emotional issues can be difficult. Often, when feelings are involved, there is little chance for an open discussion. Time is a great tool if used properly. Since nobody is good in a crisis, a parent should never back another parent into a corner when it comes to a decision about a child. It never works.

In the early days of my separation, it seemed as if every discussion between me and my son's mother resulted in a quarrel. No matter how carefully either one of us presented the decision, it always seemed to lead to a fight. The simple phrase, "Let me think about it," proved to be a savior in our family's discussions.

I can't even remember the "important" decision that was presented to me, but I do remember being unhappy about her solution. Desperate to avoid a fight, I told her that I'd think about it and returned the next day, better prepared for a discussion. Fight averted.

At first this seemed to work. Whenever I could feel a fight brewing, I'd ask for time to think about it, but it didn't take long for her to notice that this meant I didn't agree with her opinion. Finally, we came to another "important" decision that I can't remember, but I do remember feeling a fight was brewing. Almost out of reflex, I said, "Let me think about it."

I could see her face twist at the thought of my rebuttal the next day. I assured her that her idea sounded good, but I wanted to give it some thought. Skeptically, she agreed. The next day, I returned to agree with her solution. Her relief was obvious, and we had found a solution for making decisions.

Over the years, we've perfected this approach. If there's an emotional issue that needs a decision, one of us will dump the problem before the other—emotions and all—and we'll each take time to think about it. Then, after the emotions have settled, we return for a rational discussion. As for me, I've learned to value her opinion, even if I disagree with it. It's the first opinion I seek when I have a decision to make that affects my son.

Whether married, separated, or divorced, an effective co-parent is one that can lead without exerting power or authority over their partner. Making swift decisions is less important than making the right decision. This is only possible after open discussion. A strong parent originates plans and ideas for raising a child but does not care about receiving credit or winning an argument. Opposing viewpoints should always be considered, and a good parent is one who's willing to let others change their opinions.

When co-parents seem locked on two sides of an argument, they can often be blind to any form of compromise that might be better in the long run. Compromise means progress, but this takes practice. Often, uniting the family is more important than any single decision, no matter how big it might seem at the time.

Once unified, the family can finally focus on its most important purpose: to raise confident, secure, and healthy family members. In some ways, the divorced family actually has a benefit in this area. Without those everyday challenges caused by cohabitation, shared space and daily living, divorced co-parents can focus on our common purpose—raising a child together.

In my family that meant that anything that didn't have to do with raising our child was none of my business. I had to learn to separate those issues that didn't have anything to do with my son with those other, confusing topics that can veer us from our co-parenting journey. To be successful, I had to be willing to do anything that was necessary for my son's mother—even if it was inconvenient for me. I also had to be willing to ignore anything that applied to my "ex." Sometimes it still takes every ounce of energy I can muster to mind my own business or sacrifice my wishes when it comes to those outside issues like relationships, careers, and extended family, but the effort always pays off. If I only concern myself with issues pertaining to my child, it keeps me from veering off into dangerous territory, arousing jealousy, competition, or judgment.

Especially in the beginning, there were frequent mistakes and setbacks, but once I fully committed to this ideal I was able to move toward it. Many co-parents find themselves in arguments about significant others, in-laws, work issues, parenting styles, and personal decisions that, when honestly reviewed, have nothing to do with actual co-parenting. Justifying a connection with these unconnected issues is the source of most family disagreements.

Sometimes, there is an overlap between the outside world and the family unit. When having these discussions, it's best to focus on how it affects the child. It takes some practice, but it's never helpful to focus too much on the other household or the other parent. Often, on closer examination, I can usually find that my problems are more concerned with my ambitions, my standing in the family, and my security than they ever are about my child's. Usually, these issues are better discussed with trusted people outside the family unit who would be understanding but unaffected by the situation. To be most fruitful, those conversations should focus less on the other parent or the child and more on how the issue is perceived by me. Solving the emotion is usually more important than controlling the situation.

The family has to come first if everyone is going to succeed—especially the child. That means that parents must work together. Again, unifying the family has to be the ultimate goal. With practice, this new attitude begins to come naturally. Those moments of peace that were so elusive before become common.

Equality has to become a top priority, and this is necessary no matter what the courts say. Custodial parents can feel emboldened at times. Homes can become protective forts, and contractual agreements can be wielded as weapons. This works against any hope for family unity. Noncustodial parents can often feel powerless, excluded, and inferior. Making healthy decisions as a family requires an understanding of this power dynamic, whether it is real or imagined on either side. Conflicts can stem from competing ambitions intensified by power dynamics. Security issues can be aggravated quickly by arguments over status, rank, or social standing. Children don't count minutes or measure love on a scale. Neither do healthy parents.

As the custodial parent, my best decisions were made when I considered my son's needs first, his mother's second, and mine last. The biggest challenge was time. Quick decisions were often my most selfish. Agreement isn't always possible, but it should always be the goal. That requires conversation and voting. Everyone has to be able to participate. Everyone has to be able to make decisions, and everybody must be able to question those decisions down the road. If it doesn't involve anything immoral or harmful to the welfare of the child, this is a co-parenting issue not a legal one.

Differences common to most families can seem bigger when there's separation. Co-parenting challenges often stem from different family histories, parenting methods, and approaches. How does a broken family mend? How do parents overcome differences in parenting styles, competitions between households, and long-standing hurts in order to function as a whole?

Allowing differences to continue between households is an important step for overcoming competition between them. There's nothing constructive about jealousy or competition. In the early days of my divorce, it seemed that there were all sorts of things that happened in the other household—real and imaginary—that seemed to spark jealousy in me. It seemed like I experienced a moment of crisis every day because I was viewing everything that happened in his mother's house through a lens of jealousy and competition. I have come to understand that this sort of thinking is fairly common.

Every successful milestone that occurred in the other home felt like a threat to my peace of mind and my parenting skills. When my son reached a milestone during a visit with his mother, it seemed to threaten my own self-esteem. When she was able to manage a successful relationship, it threw any loneliness or resentment that I was feeling into crisis. Any success she had—at work, at love, at parenting—forced me to focus more on my failures or inadequacies.

Equally, any failure in her house was seen as a major accomplishment in mine. It is amazing how a mind fueled by jealousy can relate two unrelated issues such as her successes and my failures. This sort of competition can eat away at the family and can hurt a child's development in both homes.

Each parent has to be free to parent in whatever style and in whatever way they want unless it affects the entire family or causes actual harm to the welfare of the child. If two parents are going to work together to raise a child, they should be free to live and play in any way they choose when they are in their own homes. To make this possible, I had to adopt a simple perspective. I had to be easy on her and tough on me. I could not criticize anything that happened in the other home unless it directly affected my home or endangered the welfare of our child. Conversely, I had to be sure to include my son's mother in any decision I made in my home that had the potential to affect her home positively or negatively. Once again: I had to be easy on her and tough on me.

This doesn't always seem fair, but if peace of mind and family unity are the goals, this is the only perspective that seems to work. If I was honest with myself, I found that few issues in her home needed to be discussed. I also found that I was able to share more freely the successes and failures that occurred in my home. Once at least one parent embraces this position, both parents become safe to experiment in the process of trial and error. Free from criticism, both parents are free to discuss their successes and failures openly. It becomes easier to avoid gossip and arguments or to impose boundaries. I was able to overcome those self-esteem and security issues that block communication between households. I began to appreciate her successes and support any setbacks. The wall between us began to come down. We began to co-parent.

The biggest source of competition seemed to center on our different parenting styles. How does one deal with different rules and routines in different households? How can these parents remain unified if their approaches differ? In order to work together, do these styles have to be compatible? Sure, it can be helpful if a child's routines are consistent, but I found that this wasn't absolutely necessary. In fact, coping with different routines and parenting styles can provide a healthy opportunity to work on unhealthy demands about plans, expectations, and schedules.

To cooperate with my co-parent when our approaches seemed to be incompatible, I found that I had to adopt a simple approach. When he was at someone's home—whether it was his mother's or mine—my son had to follow that person's rules. When he was at his mother's home, her rules and routines applied, and I would support them. When he was at my house, my rules applied. To keep it simple, I expanded that idea even further. The simple rule was to follow the authority wherever he was. At school, he would follow his teacher's rules. At the homes of family and friends, they would have the final say. It created some funny and awkward moments when he would ask a friend for permission to do something that I wouldn't ordinarily approve of—like eating a snack that I wouldn't allow at home. My friend would look to me for approval, but I'd just shrug my shoulders and say that it was up to them. This was easy to do because I never found myself in somebody's home if I didn't trust them. By giving them authority, it helped my son to forge relationships and have simple conversations with people other than me. It helped me, too. The more I was able to relinquish control, the less I struggled with authority issues.

The bottom line is that it helped me to be consistent with

my son even when the rules were inconsistent. It simplified the approach. It helped me to support my son's mother, my son's teachers, and my friends and family whether I agreed with their approaches or not. Sometimes, I even found that their approaches worked better than mine. Most importantly, it helped me to avoid unnecessary conflicts and helped keep me from being too controlling when it came to my son.

Of course this wasn't easy, but divorce and separation never is. Like everything else, overcoming dysfunction takes practice, along with trial and error. Bad parenting decisions are usually those that are made in haste when clear thinking is clouded by emotion or confusion. Full agreement isn't always possible, but it should always be the ultimate goal. Good decisions should not be made based on power dynamics or custody. Open conversation and willingness to compromise lead to a unified front.

Healthy co-parenting requires a partnership in both major and minor decisions, along with mutual trust and respect. When divorce, separation or dysfunction clouds this relationship, families have to revisit their process for decision-making and commit to family unity. Parenting is about being loving, honest, unselfish, and straightforward. The biggest challenge to this is our emotions.

# CHAPTER EIGHT

*The Speak Easy: Communication and Language*

Communication is a fundamental tool for parenting. It is absolutely essential that parents connect with their children on a personal level, so that they can freely express ideas and share knowledge. Parents share stories, communicate thoughts, and model coping skills. It happens every day in formal and informal ways. With babies and toddlers, we carefully select books that play with language and draw simple conclusions. As the child matures, so do the conversations. These conversations can be playful, instructive, serious, or intimate. Words help to shape a child's world.

But with my son's autism, this wasn't just an obstacle. It felt like a barrier when he was young. He avoided eye contact, and he wasn't physically attached to the world around him. He did not show any inclination toward spontaneous speech. He didn't go through those normal phases where he mimicked sounds or speech. He didn't point at and label objects, and he wasn't focused on playing, watching television, or reading books. Although he has made great progress, these skills still don't come easily to him.

I struggled to make connections, too. I had trouble reaching out to him. It was nearly impossible to capture his attention. No matter how hard I tried, I couldn't seem to find anything that would spark his curiosity. Science may someday understand the autistic mind, but medicine has yet to learn the complex combination for unlocking the language vault. Autistic studies are in their infancy, so any realistic advancements toward understanding the autistic mind are probably a long way off. As a parent, I had to admit that I knew even less about my son's condition than those experts.

Sure, I had day-to-day experience surviving life with an autistic child, but that didn't give me any ability to understand what was going on in his mind. Consequently, we struggled to establish those intimate connections that parents form with their children. Without words, the easiest thing to communicate is loneliness and isolation. We were living in the same house, but we weren't really living together.

We were fortunate to have caring doctors, teachers, and specialists who took an interest in my son from an early age, but it did little to help our everyday home life. Long before specialists landed on his diagnosis, there were preschool helpers in our community. They converged on my son, trying to kick-start social development and learning. There were some small successes amid the frustration of frequent setbacks, but it did help to finally have access to some resources in our household. They sometimes offered new tools for refocusing his negative behaviors along with some fundamental language exercises, but their main focus was on education and the social skills needed for the classroom.

Simple, everyday communication still seemed out of reach. He did like certain books, but only to satisfy his routines. Adding new stories, talking about spontaneous topics, and finding common ground wasn't really possible without tremendous effort, and even then it didn't seem to be very meaningful for either one of us.

Handling meltdowns was the top priority in our household, and it felt as if my full-time job was managing those breakdowns. As he got older, his fits became so physical that he was a danger to himself and everyone around him. At his school, these tantrums would often require two or more trained adults just to contain. At home, without a team of experts, it was even worse. Injuries were common. He hurt a pair of teachers at his first school. Even when he was a small child, he injured me several times.

My son's preschool teachers, along with a number of behavioral experts, taught me safeholds, de-escalation techniques, and safe methods for self-defense. We developed escape plans that were as well rehearsed as elementary school fire drills. There were many abandoned shopping carts in those days, along with many inquisitive looks in the parking lot. We developed complex mirroring techniques. I learned to match his emotions and mirror coping methods. Over time, I developed the discipline and stamina that the outside world sees in parents of special needs children, but it was all superficial. Our lives became a subtle and complex battle to control behaviors. Controlling unruly behavior was my primary objective, and our success was limited, at best.

On the other hand, I was so focused on avoiding those mental breakdowns that I was learning how to listen to a child that doesn't speak. Like most special needs parents, I learned to identify those nonverbal cues like breathing, posture, and body language that would signal the next tantrum. Like most parents of special needs children, I seemed to develop a sixth sense when it came to his behavior, and there were many times when I was able to head off a tantrum or deflect some jarring emotion before it swelled into crisis. But, just as my confidence was growing, there would inevitably be some sort of unforeseen crisis that would remind me that control was an illusion.

Because his rage was so uncontrollable, it was necessary to be constantly on guard. I had to proactively address any new stressors before they took hold. Out of necessity, we learn to identify those subtler emotions like anxiety, confusion, uncertainty, and vulnerability that can build into anger, fear, or sadness. If any of these are left to fester in my son, they can build into rage and manifest as a tantrum. Under the right circumstances, even positive emotions like joy, contentment, and enthusiasm can cause confusion and can escalate into an outburst.

Even though most people can handle a certain amount of worry or confusion before it becomes overwhelming, that isn't the case with a child who struggles with language and social skills. As I studied my child, I noticed that a simple worry would quickly escalate into rage. He would focus on a simple challenge, and I could actually see it build into an eruption. Even those simple challenges like hunger, fatigue, or pain would grow into a crisis for my child. Over time, this leads many special needs parents to hover over our children like K-9 police units sniffing out problems. We act as if we're at a crime scene, holding back the crowd, shouting warnings, and protecting the evidence. This can be exhausting, and it is ultimately ineffective. Perhaps there's a better use for those bomb-sniffing skills? Of course there is.

For experienced special needs parents, it isn't what to talk about that creates problems. It's how to talk to the child that poses a challenge. How do we make connections with children who don't seem to want to connect? How do we find common ground? Luckily, that's not as difficult as it might seem at first. The key is found in our own daily reviews.

Those emotions that I was so good at spotting in my child were the very same ones that were present during my moments of crisis. Those subtle emotions that were driving my son toward his next meltdown were the very same ones that were sowing seeds for my troubling moments. Sure, I had a higher threshold before my meltdowns, but that's because I had language skills and life experience that my son didn't. I had been looking for common ground, and that's what those emotions turned out to be. I still didn't understand his condition, but I certainly could identify with his feelings. As I became better at understanding these emotions in me—along with the causes, conditions, and solutions—I finally had something to offer him. I could use my language skills to help him overcome his emotional issues. As it turned out, those everyday frustrations proved to be our common ground.

I will always remember the first breakthrough I made. It happened after my son returned from a weekend with his mother when she was battling a severe cold with a fever. Any other parents would have switched weekends, but with a calendar savant that option was out of the question. His mother did the best she could. This is the strength of most special needs parents, enduring situations that would overwhelm the most hardy of people because it's in the best interests of our children. In retrospect, I was the one who failed our son.

When I dropped him off at his mother's house, I told him that she was sick and cautioned him to be on his best behavior. At that time, he didn't speak more than a word or two, and he rarely reacted when I spoke to him. I don't know why I said this. I was probably trying to be helpful (and feeling a little bit guilty that I was handing him off to a sick parent).

I was worried all weekend, but my worry seemed to be over nothing. When his mother dropped him off on Sunday afternoon, she reported perfect behavior. There wasn't a single meltdown all weekend. Our son was calm and happy for two days, and she was able to rest.

My relief was short-lived. The moment the door closed, my son exploded into a fit of rage. He attacked me, punching and kicking. He screamed. He clawed at my face. Out of sheer instinct, I scooped him up, ran to his room, and closed the shades. We climbed onto his bed, and we went through my entire checklist for mitigating a crisis.

At one point, I said something about his mother being sick, and I could feel him stiffen up. "Is that what's bothering you?" I asked. His reaction was very subtle. If I hadn't been looking for it, I probably would have missed it. He sighed. I felt like he'd opened up a window, and I was finally able to see inside.

It was clear to me that his weekend was not as peaceful as either one of his parents had initially thought. Most likely, he had been wrestling with his emotions all weekend as he struggled to process the fear and anxiety that come from having a sick parent. He had managed to stuff his feelings like I'd asked him to do, but everything came tumbling out once he let down his guard at my front door. My well-meaning words of caution at the beginning of the weekend created a dense burden that he shouldered for two days.

Of course I apologized, even though I'm sure he didn't understand me. I cradled him in my arms, and he eventually calmed down. "Mommy is going to be alright," I said. "We all get sick from time to time."

Over the next few hours, I tried to reassure him. Trying to let him know that I understood what he was feeling, I began to recount a story from my own childhood. As I spoke, I could feel him calming in my arms, so I let the whole story come spilling out. In soft tones, with very simple words, I told him about my own experiences with a sick parent. When I was around his age my mother had spent a whole year battling cancer. She was in and out of hospitals, and I was full of fear and insecurity.

I shared my memories about how it felt, what I was thinking, and how I coped. I spoke about the worry I felt when my mother was sick. I spoke about the anxiety and confusion. I spoke slowly and simply, choosing my words carefully and focusing more on the way I felt than the details of the situation. He seemed to respond the most when I was talking about how powerless I felt about my own mother's sickness. I couldn't wish her well any more than he could. I told him that I didn't understand most of my emotions at the time, but that I had developed some tools as I got older. I talked about confusion, and explained what that is.

I still can't be sure that he understood anything I was saying, but I couldn't deny the way it was affecting him. His temper tantrum had stopped. His whole demeanor had calmed, and we lay together on the bed as I told a story that I had never told anyone else. It seemed to be helping us both.

I was basically doing a crisis inventory out loud and in real time. I was searching for those long-forgotten emotions. I was asking myself what those emotions felt like, what caused them, and how I would deal with them today. I touched on all the plans, expectations, and routines that were impacted, along with how I reacted. I talked about all the ways my social life was confused and upended. Visits to the hospital kept me from playing with my friends. Days were spent with extended family or friends, while my parents handled the doctor's visits and treatments. I talked about loneliness, fear, and anxiety. I told him about my insecurities—for me and my mother. I talked about how it affected my father, my brothers, and the rest of our family. Worst of all was the fact that nobody would tell me what was going on or what to expect. I heard them talking in hushed tones with faces full of worry, but they told me as little as possible. I talked about the things I did well, and the ways I acted poorly.

I realized somewhere along the way that he was still listening. More importantly, a calmness had settled over him. I don't know if he understood everything that I was saying or if he was just calmed by the tones. At the moment, it didn't matter because we were obviously connecting.

I kept my conversation on simple terms. When he seemed to identify with something, I'd dwell on it. When it didn't seem to resonate, I quickly moved past it. In that way, I let him direct the discussion. I found that the feelings were more important than the details.

Once we were both calm, I steered the conversation to his own mother's sickness. I assured him that it would pass. I told him that we would all be OK, and it wouldn't have any lasting effects on any one of us. I also promised that we would check in with her every day until she felt better, and we would ask her if she needed anything.

At the end, I told him that there was little else we could do … except love her. I told him that we could say a prayer for her if he wanted, and he did. So there on the bed, with my arm around him, we said a simple prayer, "God, help Mommy." A few minutes later, we left his room and spent a quiet night doing our normal Sunday night activities.

Over the next couple of days, we continued to check in with his mother. When we saw her, we talked about her progress. Every night, I reviewed our day, and we talked about his mother. Usually, he'd follow it with, "God, help Mommy."

Looking back on it, I don't think it matters if I over-explained, under-explained, or whether I was right or wrong. For the first time, I was able to connect with his problem, use my language skills to put his feelings into words, and model solutions. It wasn't a coincidence that he didn't have another meltdown while his mother was recuperating, and things eventually returned to normal.

But I had changed. This spontaneous conversation between father and son was one of the most intimate moments that we had ever shared, a simple conversation about dealing with a sick parent. He needed me, and I was there. His crisis was easily averted, and mine never came to be. This was a good parenting moment. I wasn't concerned about my plans for the day, my social life, my money problems, or anything else but my son's worries about his mother. There were no hidden motives. I wasn't trying to calm him or change his behavior. I was just trying to share, honestly, my own experiences with a sick parent. It was just what the doctor ordered.

The importance of our conversation hadn't yet occurred to me, but I can now see why it was so effective. At the time, it was purely accidental, but I've learned to recreate the conditions necessary to spark this sort of communication with a young man who struggles to understand his feelings and the world around him.

The most important aspect was that he had my full attention. I wasn't trying to control his behavior. I was focused on him and responded to his feedback. Language wasn't my son's go-to communication method, so those other forms of communication were just as important—maybe more so. My tone, my gestures, and my genuine caring were as much a part of the conversation as the words I used. I had taken the time to ensure that our conversation occurred in a quiet, relaxed environment with no distractions. I was speaking slowly, softly, and simply. I wasn't in a rush, and was following his lead. I wasn't lecturing or talking down to him. I was simply sharing my own experience and trying to identify with him. I focused on my feelings and my memories, but I worked hard to relate them to his problem. I didn't over-explain, and I offered him a solution with a simple prayer. Most importantly, I kept it as short as possible.

We have had many conversations since that first one, and these are the conditions that have proven to be most effective. Lectures don't work. Telling him what to think or feel doesn't create an intimate moment. Our most constructive conversations are usually built on a simple connection and a shared experience. Instructing him isn't the purpose. Controlling his behavior isn't my main ambition. Yet, both of these things were by-products of a more effective form of communication.

The full implications of our conversation weren't immediately apparent. My son was still unable to express much more than anger, but this was a good beginning. Since that day, we began to talk about those other emotions when we encountered them. We talked about confusion, disappointment, guilt, anxiety, and excitement. I matched his feelings with stories from my life, breaking down all my insecurities, social issues, and ambition problems, so that he could relate. I started to speak to him on his level, and it worked.

I finally found common ground with my son. I still didn't understand his condition. I couldn't identify with his language problems or the way his mind processes information, but I could understand his emotional turmoil. It was the crisis that we had in common, not his condition. I didn't always have the answers, and I admitted that, too. But for the first time in our lives, we were in it together. We were partners, growing together.

Rather than fighting his next crisis, I decided to embrace it. Rather than trying to stifle his meltdowns, I decided to lean into them. What followed was a long process of trial and error, but that decision to focus on what we had in common was the first building block for communication. When he was in an emotional crisis, he lashed out at me and everything else around him. After a while, I became sensitive to his outbursts because they presented me with an opportunity to connect with him.

Everything about this approach wasn't easy. Since we were connecting during tantrums, he began to aim his anger directly at me even more than he did before. On the other hand, it was clear that we were connecting, and the discussions were helping. He'd even have moments of eye contact, which was very rare in those days. At the very least, he was finally focused outside of himself. If I could safely enter that space, communication was possible.

A short while later, we were at a friend's backyard party. We were enjoying a day with our friends, swimming in the pool, and listening to music. My son discovered the hot tub, and he was perfectly happy, giggling every time the bubbles began. It was a perfect day for both of us until one of the hosts—I'll call her

Sue—had to excuse herself because she wasn't feeling well. She went inside the house to rest but insisted that the party continue.

I am blessed with good friends. Everyone insisted that my son and I continue to enjoy the pool while they pitched in to help the host. Friends kept checking on Sue to share updates. She even made an appearance a little later to show that she was feeling a little bit better.

The atmosphere at the party returned to normal, but my son soon began to show signs of stress. He began to fidget. He became anxious. He didn't want to sit in the hot tub or swim in the pool. It quickly became apparent to me that a meltdown was looming, so we cut our visit short and escaped to our home. Once there, I ushered him up to his room, pulled down the shades, and we practiced slow breathing on his bed.

He took a deep breath and sighed. "God, help Sue."

That's when I fully realized that we had made a big advancement in our communication. It was clear to me that my son made the connection between his mother's illness and Sue's, so we began to talk about our friend. I explained that it wasn't a serious illness, and that she would probably feel better by the next day. We made plans to follow up with her to make sure that she was feeling improved, and I slowly steered the conversation toward other topics as his emotions returned to normal. Eventually, we left his room to spend a quiet afternoon together, and Sue felt much better when we followed up with her the next day.

Once again, my son and I were able to find common ground and have a simple discussion. Once again, he had my full attention. I wasn't trying to control his behavior. I was focused on him and his feedback. His room provided the perfect relaxed environment with no distractions, and we spoke slowly, softly, and simply. His nonverbal feedback guided our discussion. I didn't over-explain, and I reinforced his solution—to pray for our friend and follow up the next day.

This was a huge breakthrough for us. For the first time, it felt as if we were working together instead of battling each other. Solving emotional problems isn't a special needs issue. This is a common problem for most parents and children that was just compounded by his special needs. If we could find common ground, I could help mentor him through emotional turmoil by using my feelings and experiences to guide him through his.

I felt as if someone had swung open a door for us. That conversation about a sick mother became the first benchmark for every conversation that followed. Whenever I'm feeling something uncomfortable, I talk to him about it. Whenever I notice him struggling with an emotion, I try to identify it for him. I try to be honest about my feelings, and I try to talk through my decisions and actions. I think it helps me as much as it helps him.

I have yet to find a perfect format for these communications. Sometimes, they can be scheduled. Sometimes, they must be spontaneous. Often, it is impossible to be fully prepared, but there are a few things that I've found necessary for good communication.

As quickly as possible, I identify the emotion, along with a time that I struggled with it—the more recent, the better. Then, I talk about the underlying causes and conditions—the insecurities, social issues, or ambitions—that sparked the emotion. I speak freely about the challenges I have had dealing with the same emotions, and I try to provide some choices or solutions that work. It's important to get to the point quickly. If not, any emotion might quickly morph into anger.

Most importantly, I talk about myself instead of lecturing or instructing. Using simple "I" statements, like "When I get angry …" or "When I'm confused …," can open up a meaningful conversation.

To be prepared for these conversations, I doubled down on my own daily inventory. By recognizing my own emotional problems, I was able to better support him in dealing with his own. Most of the time, I can talk about specific failures and successes. I can talk about what I do understand and what I don't. The good news is that I don't have to be an expert myself. There has never been harm in admitting that I don't know the answer. In fact, it often provides us with a better opportunity to work together and find solutions as a team. I no longer feel the need to avoid problems, and I'm no longer in a rush to solve them. I've become more patient and tolerant because I've learned that the journey is more important than the destination.

Now, when someone presses my buttons, and I think it will help him, I talk about it. When something presses his buttons, I try to identify with him. We talk about the whole spectrum of emotions—good and bad. I share when I need help and how I'm going to find it. I've become more self-aware, and so has my son. I've found that when we talk about those feelings, like sadness, confusion, hurt, anxiety, and guilt, they are less likely to build into a crisis in him—or in me. As our conversations increased, his outbursts decreased. That wasn't a coincidence.

Sometimes a problem sparks a long conversation. Sometimes it's a very short one. Usually, it depends on him and his reactions. Our relationship is no different than any other parent and child. Sometimes he wants my help, and at other times he doesn't. Over time, he's become better at asking for help, and I've become better at listening to him. We've both become better at identifying and dealing with our emotions, and it's become one of our greatest strengths.

I have learned to make conversation a priority, and that's easy to forget when a child struggles with language. Learning to develop open and comfortable communication is critical if we want to develop relationships that build confidence, self-esteem, and cooperation. Of course, conversations pose unique challenges for families with special needs. Specialists and teachers can prove to be valuable resources, but don't be afraid to develop your own style.

Set aside time and practice. I found it helpful to return to a troubling moment later in the day to go through it again. Make sure to be positive about what was done well and not punitive or judgmental.

There are some universal principles that help to foster communication skills. It helps to pause often and think about what you are going to say next. During those pauses, it's useful to focus on the child's verbal and nonverbal responses. Be prepared to repeat yourself, change directions, or respond to their feedback. Use short sentences and simple words. Talk about their options, and let them decide. Giving them agency in their own life is an important principle for all parents, and that poses a challenge for all special needs parents. It's so easy to justify controlling behavior or to underestimate a child's abilities, but it's not helpful in the long run.

Of course, knowing when to quit a conversation is just as important as knowing when to start one. Let them end the conversation—even if you are not finished. Remember to wind down the conversation nonverbally. My son liked to sit in silence after a long talk, so it's important to let him.

I wish that I could say that a switch was flipped, but real change takes time. On the other hand, that discussion marked another turning point in my relationship with my son. I learned how to detach. I began to develop better strategies as I became more self-aware. Other people's opinions mattered less as I focused on my son's needs rather than my own. Over time, his tantrums began to level out. Our communication skills began to improve. I began to develop real patience, love, and tolerance during those moments of struggle, and we learned to appreciate the calm periods in between. Common sense solutions worked for us, and it could work for others.

# CHAPTER NINE

*Life Events: Vacation, Death, and Love*

---

Once communication is established, even at a basic level, it opens the door for all sorts of things that seemed impossible before. Many special needs families live in a sort of self-imposed isolation because it's overwhelming to imagine any trip outside the safety and security of the home. With new people, new surroundings, and new environments, the outside world can present all sorts of triggers for meltdowns, panic attacks, and difficult behaviors. In trying to avoid these episodes, well-meaning parents can actually limit a child's potential to explore the world.

Every parent goes through this stage of protection, not just special needs parents. Babies must be tended to constantly. During this first stage, parents need to be overprotective. At this point, it's a matter of survival. A baby's physical security depends on the attentive parent. We hover, interact, and help make sense of a baby's environment.

This continues, to a lesser and lesser extent, as babies begin to crawl, walk, and explore. Parents still need to hover and protect the child from simple dangers as the child begins to understand the environment. But at some point, a healthy child is allowed to explore further on its own. As the toddler becomes a young child, parents step back again, allowing the child an opportunity to learn through trial and error. At each phase of development, from baby to young adult, a parent learns to step back and let go a little more. As the child matures, the parent does, too. The role shifts slowly from protection to support as the healthy child grows into an independent adult.

This may not be as true with a special needs child, especially if there are mental or emotional limitations that extend through each developmental stage. As the child struggles, so does the parent. Toddlers become young children, but the simple dangers still persist. Consequently, the parent continues to hover and protect long after those early stages of development. Because it can be easily justified, this protection phase can last much longer than is needed or is even helpful. It sometimes creates quite an unhealthy codependence between parent and child. Driven to the extreme, without any real intention to do so, parents can become manipulative, overprotective, and controlling. We can place almost absurd limits on our children as if we were handling a fragile antique.

When he was an infant and a toddler, my son didn't learn from his mistakes as easily as a typical child does. He didn't have a normal understanding of his environment, and he could easily put himself in danger. Once he lost contact with an adult, he would charge forward like Peter Pan with no recognition of the dangers ahead and no connection with anybody left behind. He was an escape artist, and if you blinked you missed him. Once free, he bolted like an escaped convict through a hole in the fence. He was surprisingly fast and would seize on any opportunity for escape.

Even at a very young age, he had an uncanny ability to open locked doors, getting past child safety gates, and scrambling over any barrier that blocked his path. There was a complete failure to identify any perils such as getting hit by cars, falling, or drowning. This disconnect continued long after the baby and toddler stages. So, as a parent, I was forced to hover and protect him long after one would a typical child. If I let go of his hand, he would run. If I looked away for a moment, he might cross a busy highway. If the car door was unlocked, he could escape from his child seat and hop out at a red light. Once, he escaped from a kiddie pool and raced across a busy street. While he slipped into a crowded restaurant, his panicked parent was searching frantically in the wrong direction. These very real dangers and frightening episodes served to reinforce my need to protect him physically, and it helped to justify my overprotective nature.

The real problem came when I used my fear-driven reasoning to justify my role as a protector in his emotional and intellectual life. I found myself hovering during those rare social opportunities, speaking for my son to facilitate his interactions. I would find myself taking over tasks for him that he was perfectly capable of doing. It was harder for him to use utensils, so I'd make sure that he had finger foods instead. I would structure all his activities, hover over all his play, and eventually found myself doing things for him instead of allowing him to struggle and learn. With good intentions, I had become another obstacle to his development.

By trying to protect him emotionally and mentally, I had effectively built a protective wall around him. I had made it nearly impossible for him to explore or make mistakes. By trying to protect our children, we can actually become one of the biggest challenges that they will have to face.

It's easy to justify this control by pointing to the inevitable meltdown or emotional crisis. The effort it took to deal with those emotional and mental issues helped justify any means to avoid them. In this way, special needs parents can often make our children overdependent, and that is not the role of any good parent. This sort of parenting does little to prepare the child for an independent adult life. True, a special needs child may never become fully independent, but a parent's job is to help them become as independent as possible based on their abilities and judgment. It is a parent's job to prepare a child to overcome obstacles, not to shield them from these obstacles.

There is an even bigger danger to hovering over our children as they grow. As a parent becomes more controlling—even with good intentions—the child becomes more rebellious. Often, by justifying my controlling behavior in those emotional or mental situations, I would bring about those very meltdowns and tantrums that I was trying to avoid.

That isn't to say that parents should not protect their children at all. Of course safety concerns must be treated seriously. My son might have died had we not hovered physically during his escape phase. We weren't perfect. He escaped at his mother's house, with his father at the mall and a museum, and at countless other times during the many years it took to help him understand physical boundaries and safety.

Even as he approaches adulthood, he is not always able to be fully independent outdoors. The key is to determine when protection is actually needed and when it helps to back off. This is different for every child. The good news is that specialists and teachers can be great allies for establishing protocols to address these concerns. The other good news is that most of our failures don't result in hazardous moments.

In our family's situation, that hard line only needs to be drawn in my son's physical environment when we are outside the home. When it comes to his emotional and mental life, I had to learn to control my protective impulses. My job was to help him overcome the inevitable pain, not avoid it. Communication made that possible. Rather than embracing the role of protector, I had to adopt the role of mentor.

As our communication skills grew, this became more possible. Over time, I was able to step back and let him explore relationships, his emotions, and those unavoidable challenges that come with independence. Like all children, he experienced embarrassment, hurt feelings, unrequited love, and the death of close friends and family. As hard as it is to see any child struggle with these normal emotional challenges, it can be heart-wrenching to see a special needs child grappling with these still complex emotional challenges. It was only important that I help him to identify his feelings before they escalated into rage. Then, I could use my own experience to show him how to deal with these emotions in the way that we outlined in the chapter about communication.

Playing the role of mentor meant that I had to learn to model behavior, talk through emotions, and explore the world outside our everyday lives. It is important to push the boundaries when appropriate and to try new things whenever possible. For a special needs family, trapped in the routines and schedules of everyday living, this may seem scary, but one of the best ways to practice this was ... by taking a vacation.

It is easy to get scared away from vacations when special

needs children are involved. With so many possible problems due to the child's specific medical and emotional needs, behavioral challenges, or social issues, vacation planning for a special needs family can seem overwhelming. There can also be so many conflicting priorities between family members and siblings that it seems impossible to comprehend a family getaway. Often, special needs families opt for separate vacations or avoid them entirely. But family vacations offer a special opportunity for bonding and camaraderie, and that is especially important in special needs households where dysfunction or separation can pose seemingly impossible barriers.

Planning is everything. From selecting a reasonable destination to mapping out the trip, it is important to accommodate a child's special needs. Whether it's a trip by car, boat or plane, it is important to consider accessibility at every stop along the journey. Packing extra items, remembering necessary equipment, and planning for medical, prescription, and routine needs have to come first. In our normal, daily life I am not a planner, but I found that this was time well spent when a vacation was looming. Making lists at the end of each day, double-checking before checkout or transition, and planning the stops along the way were always time well spent. Forgetting something as simple as a special toy or favorite item has the potential to ruin a peaceful vacation.

Consulting with my son's physician was often a crucial step in preparing for a trip. It may be helpful to craft a physician's description letter for any special accommodations needed for crowded events, airports, or special venues. With a detailed list from a doctor, including specific limitations and unique needs, it can be much easier to secure any reasonable assistance and accommodations needed along the way.

With a specific list of accommodations and needs, it will help to make the trip as stress-free as possible. The list can help to make the best decisions when it comes to choosing the destination, the type of transportation, and the planned activities. Does a child require special seating? Are there special guidelines or requirements for assisting passengers with disabilities? These are questions that can often be answered long before you depart. Hotels, airlines, and travel agents can often help to identify any assistance that is available, along with any documentation that might be needed, so that you can be prepared ahead of time. Be as specific as you can about the physical, emotional, and mental limitations, and ask what documentation is required. Then, be prepared.

Of course, parents must remember that plans aren't set in concrete. Unforeseen obstacles are almost guaranteed. Once the vacation began, I had to remember that even the best-laid plans were subject to change once they went into motion. Including extra time was crucial for maintaining the patience that was needed to navigate the outside world, and I always found that the journey was just as important as the destination. Scheduling breaks was just as important as any list of accommodations or letters from doctors.

To avoid a crisis, consider the common causes: obstacles to my plans and expectations, social challenges, and security issues. Since this is a family decision, discuss it with everyone involved—spouses, siblings, and the special needs child (if possible). Is the schedule too demanding physically, emotionally, or mentally? Have you planned for problems with transitions and crowds? Are expectations too rigid or too perfect? How will the family address security concerns? What is the plan for handling embarrassment, delays, or cancellations? How do weather issues impact the plan? Is jet lag a concern? Even if it isn't, scheduling rest and downtime is important. This will also allow other family members to schedule individual activities that may not be possible for the special needs child. Even parents need downtime.

Then, once the planning is complete, remember to find moments to enjoy and relax. Sometimes families can be pleasantly surprised about the benefits of vacation. If prepared and executed thoughtfully, a vacation can help a family to overcome fatigue, stress, and chronic dysfunction.

When my son was ten years old, our family planned a vacation to a theme park, although there was no shortage of worries leading up to the trip. This was the longest trip that my son had undertaken to date, and a lot of issues needed to be hammered out. At this point in my son's development, he was still struggling with crowds, lines, and overstimulation, so we really had to question whether he was ready for everything that this trip entailed. As divorced co-parents, this inclusive family vacation raised some additional worries about lodging, cooperation, and finances. Many well-meaning family and friends said we were foolish to attempt such a big undertaking, but Jack's mother and I believed that it was going to be worth the effort. It turned out that we were correct.

Our plans were simple, and our excursions were short. My son's doctor helped us to secure the accommodations we needed. We scheduled an early start to each day with an early finish. We left big chunks of the day for relaxation together and separately. As co-parents, cooperation was our main goal, and our son's needs were the only ones that mattered. We did not plan too much. In fact, we simplified our expectations as much as possible, and worked together. Our common commitment to honesty, unselfishness, and love helped us to avoid those twisted motives and hidden agendas that emotions can evoke. We survived a transportation crisis, a few miscalculations, and a meltdown in an amusement park, but we still managed to have a fun time as a family with minimum stress. That vacation still stands out as one of our family's best shared memories, and it continues to serve as a measuring stick for cooperation and co-parenting. The ordeal was a monument in planning and execution, along with a showcase for flexibility and family leisure. I would venture a guess that there are many families, without divorce or disability, who have enjoyed less peace of mind and relaxation during their family holidays.

We may have made it look easy, but we took nothing for

granted. Our son's needs, as well as ours, were carefully considered at every step along the way. We have taken many shorter vacations—together and separately. I've always found that, with good planning, communication, and clear motives, vacations with a special needs child can be as good—or better—than a "typical" vacation.

Of course, it is impossible to plan for every life event with the detailed process of a vacation. Sometimes there isn't enough time to prepare in advance. Sometimes, by its very nature, an event can't be planned or predicted, and often these life events are impossible to avoid. The untimely death of a friend or family member is a common example of these big, spontaneous upheavals. But, if parents remain flexible and emotional issues are dealt with promptly, these events can prove to have silver linings.

Once again, communication opens doors and helps to navigate these life events. As my son matured, so did our conversations. In the early days, we spoke a lot about simple feelings, emotions, and behaviors, but there are many life events that can't be predicted. Death was a big one. Handling the emotional turmoil when a loved one dies is one of the greatest challenges that any human being can face. There can be waves of grief, sadness, guilt, and confusion. These feelings can continue for a lifetime. Memories can awaken emotions for years after the funeral.

For a special needs child that may not express—or even

understand—these emotions in typical ways or normal time frames, this can be a difficult and ongoing process. There is no easy way through it. Learning to navigate this process with my son continues to be both challenging and rewarding. In many ways, helping him to grieve the loss of friends and family has helped me more than him.

The natural impulse was to shield him from the death or distract him from his feelings, but this is nearly impossible to do when it is a close friend or relative. My son was aware of the people in his life. His connections were simple, but they were there. At a certain age, he began to schedule visits, talk about loved ones, and interact with them during visits. Because he was so adept at calendars, he was able to make plans for visits. It would be hard to explain why those visits couldn't be kept, and it definitely could spark an emotional crisis when the day finally came. I realized that I couldn't avoid the topic even if I wanted to, and that avoiding death as a topic was easier for me than it would be for him.

Instead, I chose to speak honestly and simply about the process. I spoke about my feelings, and I looked for his reactions to guide the conversation. I kept it simple and developmentally appropriate. Being direct about death is important. Using words like "passed away" or "moved on" to soften the blow could make it harder to understand. It was important to realize that a parent cannot protect a child from the pain of losing a loved one. It would be easier to stand in the waves to hold back the tide. A better goal for any parent is to help our children build healthy coping skills that

# LIFE EVENTS

will continue to serve them throughout their lives.

Before I could be any help to my son, I had to make sure I understood my own emotions and limitations. This is especially important with life-changing events like divorce, death, and loss. We are always close to crisis during these confusing, emotional times. Lack of confidence can spark self-esteem issues. Misplaced emotions can lead to conflict, and unresolved issues can hurtle us toward crisis. Once again, our inventory helps us to uncover those security issues, social problems, and unreasonable demands that can lead us to moments of crisis.

Big life changes and emotional moments can be difficult for everyone, so it is especially important that a special needs parent is aware of those emotional booby traps present during difficult times. It sometimes takes all the effort we have to ask for help from family, teachers, and specialists, but there is always a sense of relief when we do. When approached humbly and honestly, we will usually find people to be helpful and kind when we reach out for assistance. Behavioral experts, teachers, and family members can be extremely supportive in establishing a reasonable plan that takes into account a child's unique needs, limited understanding, and communication challenges.

Whether or not to attend a funeral event is a personal decision that should be determined based on the special needs of the child and the beliefs of the parents. If children don't want to go, it may not be a good idea to force them. Once a decision is made to attend a funeral, I found it helpful to discuss the event beforehand, describing what my son will see and do. We talked often. I described how the room would look, the casket or urn, and the process. We talked about the people that we will see, how those people might feel, how we can help, and what we can do. We talked about sadness, crying, confusion, and grief. We practiced how to act, and we scripted some simple phrases.

Once we arrived at the funeral, it is always important to go slow. We stop to identify pictures. I watch for signs of confusion and fear, always being ready to address them as soon as they were identified. We go at his pace, and we find that people are very helpful and understanding. These events can often feel chaotic or confusing, so it helped to have a plan. With clear understanding, good communication, and supportive assistance, these events can go smoothly.

These events almost always appear on our daily inventory because they press so many buttons for social issues and insecurities, as well as our plans, ambitions, and expectations. Wakes, funerals, and hospital visits awaken emotions in all of us, so it shouldn't surprise us that these events pose challenges to a special needs child. Sometimes, my son's emotions seemed to be out of place. He was happy at times. He would leap out of line or even giggle, but it still amazes me how my son's presence at these functions allows people to lay aside their own problems—even if it's just for a moment—to welcome him. To watch people's faces soften when they see him, to see them relax and welcome him, is a wonderful thing. He has an uncanny ability to be himself regardless of the social situation.

Often, it seemed to give our friends and family a small break from their grief as they greeted my son. With special needs children, this is often their biggest gift to everyone around them. At one family funeral, my twenty-year-old son broke the uncomfortable silence that followed the eulogy by standing, waving toward my uncle's urn, and saying, "Goodbye, Uncle Tony. I love you, and I'll miss you." It was a poignant family moment that seemed to have a positive effect on everyone in the room. During challenging emotional events like funerals, these children can be great sources of healing and strength for everyone.

At some point during the grieving process, parents must decide if they are going to discuss an afterlife, along with any religious, spiritual, or scientific beliefs that they may or may not have. Like the choice to attend or not attend a funeral, this is a personal decision. Regardless of the decision made, it is important to emphasize any comforting methods or coping mechanisms that you have discovered, taking into account the child's level of understanding and development. Once again, it is important to keep the discussion as simple as possible. Once again, teachers and specialists are often more than happy to help develop strategies for these discussions with scripting and communication aids.

Death was impossible to avoid with my son, mostly because

he loved to visit the older members of our family. Not caught up in the "normal" social landscape, without schedules peppered with school events, sports, extracurriculars, and so on, we have been able to devote a lot of time to visiting relatives. As a calendar savant, my son is able to schedule visits long into the future. My family and friends have become used to circling dates in their calendars. My son will remind them often about upcoming visits, often months ahead of the scheduled date.

During those scheduled visits, he often does little more than sit in the room with his electronics, but he likes to visit and can often surprise me. Even though he doesn't always interact, I've learned that he listens to everything. He's both blessed and cursed with an exceptional memory, so he often refers to conversations years after they occur, once he's processed the visit and developed the words to express his thoughts and feelings. It's fascinating to get insight into how he processes the world around him and what he finds important.

My son had some experience with funerals and death from an early age, but the death of a great uncle was the first in his close circle. My uncle was confined to a wheelchair for decades, and for his last few years he was caught in a seemingly endless rotation between home, hospital, and nursing home. My son enjoyed regular visits, no matter where they happened to be. Even on his worst days, my uncle would light up when my son entered the room. The two of them developed a unique relationship, and it was a privilege to watch it unfold. A special needs child can often draw the best features out of everyone he comes in contact with, and that was certainly true with my uncle.

We had encountered a number of deaths at this point in my son's life. We had lost friends, extended family, and even some children with severe illnesses and conditions. That's sad but common in special needs communities. But this death was different. We saw my uncle for weekly visits. It was a family member, and my son was clearly affected by the news of his death. Jack's first reaction was confusion.

Once again, I turned to my own inventory because I was feeling the same shock, loss, and grief. We discussed death. We talked about what it means, how I understand it, and how it confuses me. I shared my own feelings about the loss. Because we visited him regularly, my uncle's death affected our normal routines. Because my son and I loved him, it deeply affected our social lives and the lives of our family. There are also a number of mental and emotional security issues that come up when confronted with feelings of mortality. The death of a close family member checks all the inventory boxes. Everything that sparks meltdowns and moments of crisis was present—in him and me—so we talked about those boxes and discussed ways to cope with the feelings they spark.

We talked about the wake and the funeral, along with our worries, fears, and sadness. We talked every night for a long while, and now we talk about it whenever he brings it up. Years have passed, but he still brings up my uncle from time to time, and I'm able to share happy memories. We grieved together. More importantly, we navigated our feelings without any meltdowns or emotional upheavals.

Of course, this wasn't the last time or even the death that hit closest to home. In the years that followed, we've grieved the death of my father (his grandfather), a person who always seemed to rank as high as either of his parents in his life. It didn't surprise me that, at his grandfather's funeral, he brought up my uncle and some friends who had already died. He even brought up my mother, although she died before he was born. He surprised me when he listed off everyone in our family who had died, some of whom I didn't even realize we had ever mentioned around him.

For my son, the funeral is just the start of the grieving process. He regularly schedules visits to my father's grave. Being a calendar savant, he schedules visits when days remind him of an important memory with his grandfather. If a certain day falls on the same day of the week as a particular memory, he schedules a visit to the cemetery. We have visited to celebrate winter storms, family parties, and vacations, to name a few. As for my part, it doesn't matter if a visit is inconvenient. If he schedules it, we go, no matter what problem it poses for my plans, schedules, or routines.

Every time a loved one dies, my son—like all children—

shows his grief in different ways. It depends on a lot of factors unique to each relationship. By not avoiding these difficult events, he has developed a high level of emotional maturity. In many ways, he's learned to handle death and funerals as well or better than others his age despite his limits with language and expression. We've survived my brother's death, very close friends, and even some celebrities and strangers who seemed to affect him. I never know what is going to spark a reaction in him, but the process is always the same. I try to label the feelings that we are both experiencing. Then, I work to put my emotions and coping mechanisms into words for him. I stay focused on his verbal and nonverbal cues and continue to follow up as much as needed while he works through the feelings.

There are benefits for both of us. By helping him to remember the person, it helps me to do the same. By encouraging him to express himself, we have become better at understanding each other and communicating difficult events. We never avoid talking about a person who dies. Eventually, the happy stories and memories help to heal the grief. It takes time, but the effort is worthwhile. There are many resources available from teachers and specialists to therapists and ministers. As parents, it is important to acknowledge our own limitations and ask for assistance when needed.

There was only one time in our lives that this approach to life events and milestones didn't work, and that was during puberty.

This is a confusing and dangerous time for many young adults with special needs. The hormones and physical changes come at the same time as a typical teen, but the emotional and mental maturity may be much younger and less developed. This maturity-meets-immaturity creates a confusing and volatile condition, and many of his old, long-forgotten behaviors began to reemerge and amplify.

By this point in my son's life, we had developed many good strategies for coping with emotional problems. I was becoming adept at recognizing those underlying emotions like confusion, fear, and anxiety. I was usually able to intercede early, identify the emotions, and offer solutions before they built into a crisis. We were both good at talking about insecurities, social problems, and expectations. It was rare when an emotion would fester or build into anger or rage. My son's meltdowns were few and far between at home. They were lessening at school, and they were nonexistent when he was staying with his mother.

When puberty hit, all of those coping mechanisms went out the window. Fueled by hormones, those simple emotions would escalate quickly—sometimes immediately—into anger and rage. Even in those rare moments when I would recognize an underlying emotion, there was not time to intercede. The meltdowns returned in full force. They came often, and they were more severe. Because of his adult size and strength, these physical tantrums were wilder and more powerful than ever before. At school, these tantrums often took two adults to contain him. At home, it was often dangerous. He broke furniture and even injured me a few times. Once, I failed at an attempt to get him in a safehold, and he ran up the stairs with me clinging to his shoulders like a cape flapping in the wind. His tantrums were fierce and frequent. They also carried a long hangover fueled by guilt and remorse (for both of us). It was one of the few times that he needed actual medical help.

On the other hand, I had been warned about puberty for years. It almost seemed to be a mantra that teachers and specialists would trot out every time we reached a difficult stage. "If you think this is bad, wait until puberty," they would say. But they'd almost always add that once the family survives puberty, many of those difficult behaviors often disappear. Many will never return again. As it turned out, those words were prophetic. Puberty was difficult, emotionally and physically. I spent much of the time fighting off physical assaults. Even medication didn't seem to work quickly enough.

Happily, I can confess that this period was a short one, a few months, although it felt like years as we went through it. Once it passed, the dangerous behaviors quickly stopped, and they haven't reappeared. It turned out that puberty was a sort of metamorphosis for him. Breaking through the cocoon took all of his strength and emotion, but he emerged with all the color and majesty of a monarch butterfly. It was a tumultuous period, but many of his most difficult behaviors have disappeared.

The end of puberty heralded a more mature era with more

mature problems. All the effort that we had put into establishing communication skills and coping techniques began to pay dividends. My son began to come out of his shell. He became more social. He developed a better sense of humor. He still struggles, at times, with everyday conversations, but he began to develop improved social skills and stronger relationships with friends and family. Where he used to need scripting and direction, he began to develop spontaneity and initiative. He began to reach out for himself.

As his maturity increased, so did his emotions. Adolescent years are difficult for any child, but for a special needs child who might be at different stages physically, emotionally, and mentally, those adolescent years can be doubly confusing. It is usually at this stage that children begin to really understand attraction, romance, and love. Navigating this stage is difficult for any parent, but special needs children require specific guidance and understanding. Despite the progress I had made in dealing with so many of his emotions, I found myself ill-equipped initially to handle his first love. It hit him hard, and it often turned into a sort of obsession. It was all he could think about. It was all he could talk about. It drove him subtly and not so subtly. It crowded out everything else.

In that way, a special needs child is really no different than any other child. Whole sections of the library are devoted to the subject of love, while other sections are devoted to surviving teenagers. Throughout the ages, philosophers, poets and dreamers have tried to explain and solve the love dilemma. It is a common subject in most novels, plays, and movies that are often quoted, often imitated, and rarely done with ease or success. How could a divorced, confused father provide direction to a special needs child? That continues to be one of my biggest challenges, and I often fall short of my ideals.

My son's feelings about girls often verged on obsession. We had many conversations about appropriate behaviors, appropriate relationships, and appropriate speech. We had to navigate his first crush on a family member, his first crush on a schoolmate, and a number of crushes with teachers, adults, and friends. This subject dominated his teen years. There were many successes, setbacks, and unforeseen obstacles.

The turning point for us came when we were dealing with a one-way obsession he had with a special needs girl at his school. He liked her, but his feelings weren't returned.

One day, in total frustration, I told him, "You don't know what love is." (During that day's inventory, I recognized this outburst as one of my moments of crisis that day. I was tired. I had my mind set on a particular task, and his obsessive ranting proved to be the last straw. My reaction was selfish, unloving, and less than straightforward. My motive was to stop the conversation ... which, at the time, I thought I had accomplished.)

Hours passed until he finally approached me again. He shoved his tablet in front of me, and forced me to look at the screen. "Read," he said triumphantly. I quickly realized that our earlier conversation hadn't really stopped ... at least not for him. He had searched the Internet and found a Bible verse, a famous one from First Corinthians:

"Love is patient and kind. Love is not jealous or boastful or proud or rude. It does not demand its own way. It is not irritable, and it keeps no record of being wronged. It does not rejoice about injustice but rejoices whenever the truth wins out. Love never gives up, never loses faith, is always hopeful, and endures through every circumstance. Love will last forever ..."

There are dozens of different translations, but this is the one that he found during his search. I had to admit that he had me. It wasn't the first time that he'd won an argument, but it's the one that stands out most vividly. I had told him that he didn't know what love was, and he found a better definition than I could have come up with myself. Within a few days, he was reciting this passage perfectly. He knew it by heart.

For us, it wasn't about religion. We needed to find a way to discuss this challenging issue, and his ideal was as good as any I've ever found. It opened up a whole series of conversations. When his obsession sparked up, we'd talk about patience. When he would perseverate on schedules (as a calendar savant often does), we would talk about how he was being demanding, and I'd point out that it wasn't "love." We had talks about kindness, jealousy, boastfulness, pride, and rudeness. We talked about irritability, keeping score in relationships, and being honest. We talked about unfairness, hope, and endurance, and we continued to go back to that passage that he found on the Internet. It was his favorite conversation, and he adopted it as a sort of prayer when he went to sleep at night. Those discussions seemed to help both of us.

My natural inclination is to stop these difficult conversations or redirect his behaviors when the discussion is inconvenient, but that turns out to be easier for me than for him. Putting off problems often makes it harder for me in the long run as his troubling behaviors become entrenched as habits. Like most emotional issues, I learned that I had to deal with them immediately, even when they were inconvenient. I had to keep it simple. I had to use simple wording and phrases. I had to look for nonverbal cues and shift my conversation to fit his reactions. It was most effective when I explained my feelings or shared my experiences, successes, and failures. It was best when I shared what I knew and admitted my limitations. I helped script questions that could strike up conversations with love interests. We even practiced role playing, so that I could model solutions. In other words, we handle love the same way as we handle every other emotional issue we face.

It took time, along with trial and error. I took many detours, trying to distract him, change the subject, or avoid discussions entirely. There was one obsession that I just couldn't seem to figure out. He hadn't seen the girl for years, but he talked about her constantly. It distracted him from simple daily tasks like schoolwork and social activities.

He would talk about Juliet (not her name) at inopportune times. I tried to explain that she didn't love him back, and I would be met with anger. Trying to avoid the anger, I would ignore it when he would fall into his obsession and repetitive speech. Of course, that only seemed to reinforce the behavior, which made it get worse. Over time, I learned to stop when his emotions flared, and speak about times when I experienced unrequited love, but he didn't always want to make the connection. This problem began to dominate our days.

One turning point came quite by accident. He was talking about Juliet, and I told him it was OK to love her, but she didn't love him back. He began to say that. "I love Juliet, but she doesn't love me." He tried to barter. "But someday she will." Slowly, very slowly, he began to outgrow the obsession.

Those conversations helped me, too. The frequent discussions forced me to look back at some of my more troubling relationships, the demands I put on other people, and the records I keep of their wrongs done to me. I often say that my son and I grew up together. This ongoing discussion about love and relationships is a perfect example. Neither one of us can claim to be an expert, but few of us can. On the other hand, we were able to create ideals and work toward them. The rest is out of our control.

## LIFE EVENTS

The key to success, like everything else, was finding the right combination of words and experiences from my own life to help usher him through his emotional issues. It works for everything we've encountered. It works for simple emotions like anxiety, worry, and fear. It works for complex emotions like death and love. It works for simple, everyday activities, and it works for everything from highly planned vacations and events to unexpected changes in our daily routine. The only time it didn't work well was during puberty, but even that helped us work on patience and tolerance. Conversation is always the key.

We talk endlessly about upcoming vacations, birthdays, even politics and the news. If he brings it up, we talk about it. Over the years, he has initiated more conversations on more varied topics than I can even remember. Sometimes they make sense, and other times they don't. Sometimes they seem to come out of nowhere. Sometimes they resolve quickly. Sometimes they require a big time commitment to solve.

Whether they are painful, exciting or confusing, life events take preparation, courage, and persistence. Developing a plan requires empathy, honesty, and simplicity, along with proactive and timely communication. To accomplish these events may take creativity. The process might be unconventional or unique, but these milestones should not be avoided if possible. When done right, every one of these life events—even vacations—can serve a purpose. With each obstacle overcome, the family can emerge stronger, equipped with more tools for reducing stress and promoting socialization.

# CHAPTER TEN

*Surviving the -ists: Schools and Support Groups*

---

F ew parents are forced to think much about the details of their child's education. They may run into a personal problem now and then with a teacher, a fellow student, or a lesson, but when it comes to the education itself, most parents are blissfully uninvolved in the process. They don't wrestle with concepts like "curriculum" or "behavior plans." There's no thought about annual goals and objectives or how to measure improvement. Few attend workshops or town meetings where officials hammer out these concepts. Most never participate in a single vote or discussion. Curriculum decisions usually get little attention, even from local newspapers, unless there's a controversy or an unexpected shortfall. The average parent isn't an equal member of the education team. That is usually left to teachers, administrators, elected officials, and public servants. Except for during election years, most people give the educational process no thought at all.

That isn't the case with special needs families. Parents play an important role each year as educators, administrators, and specialists hammer out an individualized curriculum, but that wasn't always the process. Prior to the Civil Rights Movement, there was little thought about the segregation of special needs children or the systemic unfairness within the public school system. For the most part, special needs citizens were excluded from the educational system. Only about 20 percent of the country's disabled children were even attending school in the 1970s. The rest were uneducated or undereducated. In fact, many states had legislation that excluded children with emotional or mental disabilities from attending public schools.

Then came a flurry of legislation. Congress passed the Rehabilitation Act of 1973, which opened the door for disabled children in public schools followed by the Education for All Handicapped Children Act in 1975. It took almost three more decades to pass the Individuals with Disabilities Education Act (IDEA) in 1990 and the No Child Left Behind Act in 2004, which created the current guidelines for special education in the United States. The acts themselves are well beyond the scope of this book. It would take a team of lawyers to navigate through the volumes of legalese, along with the many Supreme Court and lesser court decisions, federal regulations, executive orders, and individual state laws. No parent, teacher, or administrator could be expected to become a legal expert on these laws, but we do have to learn to navigate them for our children.

One of the biggest challenges is to design and implement an education plan in the public school system. Under federal law, this is done under the Individualized Education Program, or IEP. Once it is determined that a child is eligible for special education, they establish a team of parents, teachers, and school administrators who are tasked with creating a unique plan for each school year. If they are physically and mentally able to do so, the child can and should play a role.

To satisfy requirements, the annual plan has to be comprehensive and tailored to the child's special needs. The IEP plan includes an individualized course of study, along with goals, objectives, measures, and testing that is specifically aimed at addressing the student's special needs. It has to take into consideration functional performance, along with any accommodations or modifications needed by the student in order to achieve success. Some guidance is given at the federal level. State regulations vary in order to satisfy requirements, but no two plans are alike. The IEP forms themselves can vary from one school to another.

It's common, especially in the early days of these meetings, that parents feel vastly unprepared and vulnerable among this team of experts. For co-parents, attendance at these meetings can create an overwhelming emotional challenge. Depending on the state of mind, a parent can feel personally attacked as each specialist presents his or her carefully prepared report, along with administered test results and future recommendations. For co-parents already struggling with competing agendas, security issues, and relationship problems, it should be no surprise that these meetings can create a tipping point for crisis.

I remember those early meetings with the IEP team. They were so uncomfortable, as my son's mother and I were ushered to our seats at a large conference table. Still smarting from our ongoing divorce and custody procedures, we were forced to sit side by side to face a sea of specialists in a scene reminiscent of King Arthur at his Round Table. The only difference was the power dynamic. As king, Arthur was in authority over his squad of knights, as each fought for resources to complete their own private quests. We, on the other hand, were subject to the local board of education representative who sat with a pen, a yellow-ruled pad, and a pile of reports from everyone in attendance—except the parents.

My son's parents were flanked by the school principal and our son's classroom teacher. There was a language specialist, a behavioral pathologist, an occupational therapist, and a number of other "-ists," each armed with a series of tests, a well-thought-out report, and an agenda. These reports were peppered with smart-sounding acronyms, obscure test references, and fragments of legalese that have to be included in order to satisfy state or federal requirements. Although every effort is made to use everyday jargon, sometimes these reports can be hard to understand, almost as if they were written in a strange language that everyone knows—except the parents. Although laws dictate that parents must receive the IEP in advance, parents often feel unprepared, vulnerable, or even judged. Parents are expected to wade through the reports and recommendations. They are expected to spontaneously discuss any limitations or challenges that weren't considered before signing off on resources, plans, and expectations.

The good news is that parents have more authority than they might think. The law is designed to ensure that parents have the right to be equal participants, make decisions, and appeal any disagreements. In fact, parents are empowered with the right to challenge an IEP through mediation, due process hearings, or litigation. Under the law, a parent's consent is needed before any plan can be implemented. To assist them in their decisions, many parents opt to bring interpreters, advocates, or outside experts to team meetings. Of course, this can all lead to more conflict and competition than anyone wants or needs.

To be most effective, a parent needs to be open-minded and nonconfrontational. This is not always easy to accomplish because parents often feel vulnerable, defensive, and confused during a discussion about the shortcomings of their child. In those early days, there wasn't a single IEP meeting where I wasn't right on the edge of an emotional crisis, but when a parent acts emotionally, it can destroy relationships within the IEP group. Hurt feelings can take time away from the group, time better spent on supporting the child. Being aware of competing agendas, strained relationships, and unsatisfied needs is the best way to avoid overreacting when those buttons get pushed—accidentally or on purpose. In other words, navigating the IEP group is no different than any other emotional situation.

Because those school meetings press all the buttons that lead to crisis, they can often reawaken issues that have long since resolved. Unrelated family dysfunctions can suddenly come to a head at an IEP meeting. Long-standing disagreements have a way of resurfacing when similar issues come up in a school meeting. These outside issues can be quite unexpected, uncontrollable, and inappropriate. A defensive parent can feel backed into a corner, and that leads to retaliation and finger-pointing—two crisis reactions that serve no good purpose in an IEP group. The only way to avoid these moments of crisis is to be aware of the underlying causes and conditions.

By putting aside our own insecurities, interpersonal problems, and unreasonable agendas, we will be better able to serve the child's needs in a rational, meaningful way. Taking an inventory before the meeting is a good way to identify those subconscious threats and lingering issues that could flare up in the meeting. Then, by continuing to stay focused on our insecurity, social issues, and conflicting agendas, we can consciously focus ourselves to embrace our true purpose—serving our child.

If parents have competing agendas, it can often reawaken past arguments. When security issues come up at a meeting—financial, mental, or emotional—it can easily reawaken past hurts. Outside issues can be easily drawn in as experts discuss behavioral problems that probe causes and conditions. Competitive issues can be further complicated when one parent brings in their own advocate, outside expert, or even a romantic partner or spouse. Jealousy, anxiety, fear, worry, and resentment can severely impair the group's purpose.

A friend of mine is a single mother, and she is co-parenting a special needs child with her child's father. They had an emotional breakup that still makes it difficult to co-parent. They live completely separate lives, but they are both committed to their child. At one IEP meeting, a long-standing issue came to a head even though it had nothing to do with the IEP itself. These two had been competing over separate agendas, and that had created a long-standing power battle in the family. They had managed to avoid fighting for more than a year as they tried to cope with their competing issues. Both parents were feeling defensive during this particular IEP meeting, but the reports seemed to poke at every issue that divided them. One spark ignited a full-blown argument, which derailed the meeting.

Later, when my friend spoke about the event, she was clearly embarrassed. More than once, she complained that her co-parent "broke up the team." It didn't matter who was right or wrong. The inappropriate argument diverted the meeting. The good news is that, after the IEP meltdown, the two were finally able to resolve the outstanding problem, and their "team" is stronger than ever. On the other hand, had the two addressed the problems before they erupted in crisis, they could have avoided some unnecessary embarrassment, turmoil, and hurt feelings. Competing agendas and power dynamics have no place in an IEP proceeding whether it is between co-parents or any other members of the group. But how do we keep those issues at bay?

Our inventory is the key. Before entering an IEP meeting, it is important that any vulnerable parent is aware of those outside pressures that can derail the meeting. Avoiding a crisis or meltdown is the first order of business because emotional sprees can cloud judgment and negatively influence decisions. Open discussion, thoughtful debate, and careful consideration are crucial if the IEP is going to be successful. Unbridled emotions make this impossible.

To survive these emotional meetings it is necessary to be conscious of those subconscious issues simmering below the surface. If we are going to avoid an irrational blank spot, it is important that we know how our plans and expectations are already threatened before we meet a new obstacle. It is important that we've already identified our insecurities before we face a new threat, and it's imperative that we are aware of our unresolved social conflicts and communication issues before an impasse is reached.

Conflict is not always avoidable, but confusion and emotional turmoil can turn that conflict into a raging war. An inventory before the meeting can help us address an issue before the boiling point. It is always time well spent.

Any IEP meeting can spark new challenges with plans and expectations. Meetings are usually scheduled during the school day, so they are often inconvenient for a parent already struggling to balance work activities, transportation issues, and time constraints. Routines that are easily accomplished in a school setting with a small army of workers seem impossible to duplicate by parents after a long workday. It's easy to feel vulnerable under these conditions.

Since these meetings highlight a child's struggles in the classroom, security issues abound. Educational goals are usually lower than a typical child of the same age. Teacher reports highlight deficits, delays, and issues in the classroom. Comparing our struggling households, rife with all the same behavioral, social, and educational issues that are peppered throughout the presentation, only seems to shine a spotlight on a parent's limitations. It is easy to get self-defensive and react by finger-pointing or blaming other members, but this isn't constructive for the group's unity.

In addition, many social challenges are on display. If there are behavioral issues, it's hard not to take it personally. Coping mechanisms that work at home might seem to conflict with "proven" educational approaches. Problems at home get carried into the school, and solutions implemented in a classroom setting can have ramifications beyond the school day.

These feelings—real or imagined—can block a parent from participating or create conflict and distrust between parents and other members of the team, and that can affect the child's chances of success. Parents are important and equal members of the team, even though it doesn't always feel like it. That is one of the main hurdles that every parent must overcome. The professionals may care just as much about the success of the IEP, but nobody worries as much or has more at stake than the parent—except the child. The experts seem to have all of the experience and credentials. They are the ones who have conducted the tests and interpreted the results. They are the ones qualified to determine the objectives, and they are the ones best able to supply arguments to support the reports that they've written. Armed with their technical knowledge and professional standing, they deliver their recommendations with confidence and reason.

It is difficult to find fault with a report when it is so detailed, so well researched, and includes such widely approved educational methods and interpretations. Since the average parent's experience is mostly anecdotal, it is hard to contradict the scientific approaches. It is no wonder why parents often feel overwhelmed at these meetings.

This begs the question, what is the role of the parent? And what is the purpose of the team? Without an understanding of the team's purpose, and the role of the parent within it, there can be no cooperation toward any sort of common goal. Without a role or a purpose, teams can devolve into competition over rival agendas, clashing environments, or limited resources. Arguments can divide a team into warring factions. If the relationship becomes adversarial, any ability to compromise or negotiate becomes impossible. Without any sense of fellowship, a troubled team is more likely to reach an impasse. Going to the extreme, a team's failure can lead to the courtroom.

Of course courts and mediation aren't always avoidable when there are valid differences in opinion. But when these disputes are a result of division, controversy, or misunderstanding within the team, the only one who's sure to lose is the special needs student.

Understanding the parent's role is the best chance to avoid a team breakdown. In many ways, this is no different than the process for a dysfunctional or divorced family. Breaking down conflicts so that the team can work toward a common goal is the same in the home as it is at the school's conference room table. A similar approach can work in both environments.

Once again, unity is the most important virtue, so adopting a positive outlook on the rest of the team members is a very important step. The family unit became stronger once I began to see my parenting "rival" as my parenting "partner," and the same is true with the educational team. Identifying everyone's strengths and expertise is only possible if I value cooperation over competition. Once this perspective is gained, the parents begin to play a central role, like a midfielder on a soccer team.

On the soccer field, midfielders aren't the ones who score the goals or protect the net, but they are the ones who make everything possible. They step back to support the defense when there's a threat. They are the ones who transition the ball to the offensive end and the ones responsible for keeping it there. They are the ones who see the whole field. They are the ones the coach turns to in a huddle. They don't score. They don't get credit for saves or shutouts, but midfielders are often the ones named as captains. Ask any soccer expert, midfielders are the key to a winning team.

The same is true of parents. The success of an IEP often depends on their ability to see the whole field of play. Specialists are usually focused on their field of expertise. Teachers are on the front lines, trying to execute the plan. Administrators, like coaches, shuffle resources in and out of the game. But parents are the ones in the midfield, anchoring the team. For an IEP team to reach its potential, the parents must play their role effectively by understanding the roles of everyone else on the team.

For some of the team members, it's easy to see their expertise. Specialists have their professional credentials and degrees. They are experts in their fields. They can help with diagnosing problems, choosing the right diagnostic tests, identifying reasonable goals, and developing the most effective plan for achieving them. Language pathologists can help with communication. Behavioral experts can help develop plans to address obstacles that hinder performance. Various professionals can be brought in to help deal with problems from motor skills and development issues to long-standing emotional trauma that stand in the way of overall success. Teachers are the experts called upon to execute the plan in a classroom environment. Administrators are tasked with the thankless burden of managing resources. Money, time, and personnel are limited, so the administrator has to balance cost with regulations and need.

The parent is the one who can make sure that the IEP is, in fact, an individualized plan. Parents are the only true experts on their child. The parent is the only one who can make sure the specialists know their child's unique strengths and needs. Parents have insight into how the child learns and plays throughout the day. Mothers and fathers understand the child's motivations and the unique challenges outside of the school day that can influence success in the classroom. Only a family member knows about problems in the home life that can hold back a child. They know the child's full history, from the beginning through the present. They are the ones who have lived with the consequences of each mistake and have firsthand knowledge of each developmental success.

Our experience is often anecdotal, but it can be just as

important as any scientific test. A parent's true purpose on the team is to make sure that the student's likes, dislikes, strengths, and unique talents are taken into consideration when finalizing an IEP. This can be critical to the success of any action plan. If there's a food plan (as there often is), what does the child like? Is there an activity they do at home that might contradict the test results? Were there similar challenges at home that were overcome and could help in the educational setting? How can the school plan be implemented or supported at home? How can the home life help prepare the child for success? Are there any resources for parents? I have never regretted asking any of these questions, and have always regretted not asking them. I have always found teachers and educational experts more than happy to answer these questions. Even when they don't have the answer readily available, they are usually happy to research outstanding questions.

Communication goes both ways. If a child is dealing with grief, loss, conflicts, personal problems, or life changes—good or bad—it can create challenges during the school day. Sharing personal information is an extremely difficult thing to do, especially if there are very real worries about how it reflects on the parent. However, it might be necessary—especially with a special needs child. Deciding when and how to disclose personal information is a challenge that must be met with courage and tact.

Asking for help, admitting our shortfalls, and accepting criticism are difficult for most people, certainly for most parents.

## SURVIVING THE -ISTS

Special needs parents are no exception. In fact, as vulnerable as we can be physically, mentally and emotionally, this can be exceptionally hard. Sometimes it can feel impossible, but the IEP meeting is an opportunity for all members of the team—teachers, specialists, and even parents—to find the resources, support, and direction they need to help the child. Take advantage of this opportunity. Sometimes IEP members can point a parent to support measures that are available in the community but unknown to the average person.

A good parent listens, challenges methods and findings with diplomacy, and shares suggestions from the perspective of the child. They are the only ones who can support the plan once the school day ends. Unlike the other members of the team, the parents aren't the ones who get the credit for the victories along the way. They are not the ones in the spotlight. They are the ones who help everyone else succeed. Their main role during the IEP meeting isn't to offer solutions, although they often do. The most successful parents ask the right questions and listen with an open mind.

There are a lot of power dynamics at play in an IEP team. Administrators are the guardians of the workplace. Parents are the guardians of the child. Teachers and specialists are in the trenches every day with their professional careers on the line. Who has authority in such a meeting of the minds? The truth is that nobody—and everybody—has authority, and that can be a difficult challenge. Everybody has good motives, an agenda, and something at stake. On the other hand, nobody can succeed on their own and nobody has ultimate authority—except, maybe, the courts. That's why conflict is such a confusing issue within the IEP team. Everyone has the child's success in mind, yet there can still be division.

Identifying and overcoming any issues that arise is crucial to the team's success. A single fight over power or standing can destroy team relationships for the whole school year or longer. When that happens, the child struggles and the IEP team fails. When it comes to the success of a special needs child, failure cannot be an option. Power dynamics have to be worked out immediately.

The same approach that worked in the family can work in the classroom. Instead of judging my actions based on my good motives, I had to be easy on others and hard on myself. I had to allow that others might have their own good motives, even if I didn't necessarily agree with them. By adopting this approach, I am usually able to see things from their perspective. In this way, I could finally see teachers, experts, and co-parents as partners rather than rivals.

Parents have to take the lead when there is confusion or disagreement. When something wasn't clear to me, I had to learn to ask follow-up questions, request clarification, or ask about their motivations outright. Conflict might be unavoidable, but confusion can always be avoided. If a professional term or acronym isn't clear, ask for clarification. If a test result seems to conflict with a parent's experience, ask about the test, how it was administered, and what it is designed to measure. Why was it necessary at this time? Are there any accommodations that might have been needed? Are there any other test options that might address inconsistencies? Were the results conclusive? What were they expecting to find from the test? Were there any surprises? Are there any explanations for why a parent's observations might differ from the test results? Is there any follow-up or additional testing needed? The answers to these questions might provide a solution that neither side had considered.

Successful teams are the ones capable of negotiation, compromise, and creativity. I'm reminded of a situation that arose with my son's education and how a compromise helped open a door. During this particular stage of my son's development, the team was struggling to find motivations that would engage my son in his studies. At home, he had demonstrated a strong interest in music and instruments. Although he didn't play an instrument, he was fascinated by them. I proposed some sort of music therapy, but the cost was too high for individualized musical lessons at the time. Plus, it didn't fit with my son's yearly goals and objectives. But one of the specialists was intrigued by my observations. He was a skilled guitar player in his personal life, and he proposed that he incorporate guitar playing into his lessons. After a short while, we abandoned the experiment when it didn't seem to spark my son's interest. However, as he got older, he began to show more and more interest in music and a form of musical therapy eventually became a mainstay in his IEP.

Even though our experiment didn't lead to immediate success, this was a good example of teamwork and negotiation that ultimately strengthened the group. It strengthened my trust in the other team members. The experiment reinvigorated a specialist in his efforts to connect with my child. Who knows? It might have even given his teachers and specialists some insight into my son's interests that helped lead his school—directly or indirectly—to eventually incorporate music into his lesson plan when he was ready. Over the years, there were many inspirations in our group. Sometimes they were met with immediate success. Sometimes, they helped to reach an eventual breakthrough. Sometimes, like my music therapy idea, it did little more than bring the team together.

Working with a special needs child is a bit like enlisting a group of safecrackers to open a vault. There can be a whole host of trial-and-error attempts. There can be immediate success or a series of failures, but when the right combination is eventually found, the door swings open for a rich and exciting discovery. The more the team works together, the better chance they have at cracking the safe. Personality conflicts arising out of twisted motives, selfishness, or unreasonable demands are the biggest obstacle to the team's success. Quarrels over competing agendas, routines, expectations, resources, or personalities have to be abandoned. The child's needs have to come before any single team member—even the parents—if the long-term goals are going to be realized.

If the group is going to be successful, everybody has to be allowed to participate in the conversation. Every person should contribute to the decision-making. Every member of the group should be allowed to challenge findings, objectives, and plans. Disagreements should be worked out by discussion, negotiation, and compromise. Decisions should strive to be unanimous whenever possible, even though it may not always be possible. Too much competition over decisions leads to poor decisions.

If the administrators are overly rigid about procedures and too stringent about resources, there can be no creativity. Teachers would have their hands tied in the classroom. Specialists would be unable to think outside the box. Parents would be unnecessary because a child's unique personality, strengths, and interests would be unimportant. On the other hand, if parents, teachers, and specialists were able to do whatever they wanted, it would be chaos. Especially in the public school setting, administrators must keep the group accountable. Federal and state guidelines need to be met, and resources must be managed responsibly. Administrators are the ones accountable to local, state, and federal agencies, along with the public. More than once, an administrator gave in to reasonable requests by the school staff and the parents, but sometimes the answer was no. A good administrator will be able to carefully explain any denials but stay open-minded to any new information that might get presented.

When teachers and specialists are closed-minded, it leads to bad meetings. If tests and reports aren't able to be challenged, parents are kept from participating. If this happens, the reports may not take into account the child's unique strengths, interests, and challenges. If a parent is excluded from the process, it leads to an adversarial relationship. Decisions are more likely to be challenged. Mistakes are more likely to be punished, and advancements made at school are less likely to be supported at home. Once again, the child is the one who really suffers.

On the other hand, if parents fight too hard to get their way in every conflict, the process can grind to a halt. When parents don't listen to specialists, they limit their abilities. When parents make too many demands for resources or time, they will make it difficult to reach a compromise or be creative. When competition between members leads to argument, small victories are always followed by bigger defeats. Nobody really wins, and the only true loser in this competition is the child.

To be successful, everybody has to be able to make decisions in their environment unless it negatively affects the child or limits another member of the group. Teachers and specialists should be encouraged to think outside the box. Parents should be encouraged to contribute ideas, and administrators should be encouraged to redirect efforts to comply with regulations while effectively managing staff and resources. Exchanging opinions, criticism, and support needs to be open and honest.

Recognizing that perfection is an unrealistic goal is very important to the success of the IEP team. Holding other members of the team to a perfect ideal is just as unfair as an expectation that a parent be perfect. In a perfect world, there would be an endless supply of money and no red tape to overcome. In a perfect world, the administrators and people in authority would never have to say, "No." In my experience, they want to avoid it as much as the parent. In a perfect world, teachers would always have the proper resources, the perfect test, the perfect plan of action, and the plan would be perfectly executed. In my experience, most of them try. They understand that perfection is an impossible goal because resources are limited. The same is true for the other specialists and experts. In an ideal world, they would all be able to devote more time, more effort, and more resources to every child in the system.

In this way, our special needs children are no different than typical students. The best we can hope for are perfect goals, good intentions, and steady improvement. The results are dependent on each team member, including the student and the parent.

When it came to my son's education, the IEP team enjoyed far more victories than defeats. We celebrated our wins as a team, and we learned from our losses. I came to appreciate the IEP, the team meetings, and most importantly, the people involved. When we worked together, everything seemed to click. Teachers offered great insight that helped me at home. Specialists made great strides in achievement and often gave me tools for the home environment. Administrators kept us on task and rarely denied a reasonable request. We had some challenges, a few disagreements, and too many victories to count.

They say that it takes a village to raise a child, and the educational team is that village.

# CHAPTER ELEVEN

*Let the Good Times Roll: Overcoming the Ordeal*

---

It may sound like special needs parents really have their work cut out for them with all the daily reviews, intimate discussions, and inconvenient decisions. It definitely takes a lot of discipline and effort to sacrifice plans to serve someone in crisis, and it takes a lot of commitment to focus on all the insecurities, social issues, and foiled plans that lead to emotional turmoil. Calculating how much time it takes to discuss problems and solutions in such detail might make a skeptic out of anyone, but the effort is worthwhile if it helps to avoid a confusing meltdown or an embarrassing tantrum. If we are honest with ourselves, it takes much more effort to deal with the fallout from a moment of crisis than the discipline it takes to do a short review of our day and have a meaningful conversation.

I have developed incredible self-awareness, but it didn't

come naturally. It didn't evolve from a great virtue or intelligence. It developed out of necessity because of the emotional roller coaster that I experienced while living with a child in crisis, a child who happened to have special needs. Parenting is one of the most difficult endeavors that any person can undertake. It reawakens emotions that we believed we had overcome for good. As our children face vulnerabilities, fear and hurt, their struggle arouses new and confusing emotions within us. As their emotional turmoil grows, it doesn't take long for it to affect the parent as well. Soon, fear and anger build into a crisis for both the parent and the child, and everyone in the household struggles. Developing self-awareness becomes an essential tool for surviving those moments of crisis and for developing healthy coping mechanisms.

For most parents, an approach that includes a disciplined daily review, awkward conversations, and an unwavering commitment to sacrifice and service will seem too drastic and unnecessary. I remember running into a good friend whose family was having a really tough time. His daughter was being bullied in school, and he was so upset that it was beginning to weigh him down throughout his day. He was losing sleep. His patience was running thin. His marriage was suffering, and he was even having frequent arguments with his daughter. Those daily clashes were keeping him up at night as he continuously replayed them in his head.

When I met up with my friend, it wasn't difficult to see that he was struggling. We had a long conversation where I shared what I had learned through living with my son. My friend could see right away that I understood what he was going through, and we realized that we shared a lot in common. I shared stories about my own family, and how social problems seemed to take on a life of their own. We talked about our children's social issues, and how it impacted us. We discussed our problems with self-esteem, power dynamics, and communication. We both admitted that, as difficult as these problems were in our lives, it was even more difficult when it happened to our friends, our family, or our children. We talked about how our social issues seemed to spark insecurities and how those insecurities clouded our judgment. We discussed how unfair situations puzzle us, and the anger that comes when people don't act the way we feel that they should.

 I could see that the discussion helped my friend, and he was interested to learn how I overcame my struggles to become so self-aware. He admitted that, like me, his emotional problems often overlapped, expanded, and soon overwhelmed him. I told him about the state of crisis that developed during the early years of my son's condition, and he admitted that he often felt that way himself. Then, I shared my solution, explaining my daily reviews, the process of understanding those underlying conditions that sparked my moments of crisis, and my commitment to sacrifice and service that seemed to help me overcome all the emotional turmoil.

 The look on my friend's face said it all. He was grateful for the conversation. It helped him on a difficult day, but he didn't see the need to go to the lengths that I described. "I'd rather have a bad day here or there," he said, "than to do all that." We both laughed and parted ways.

From time to time, I still see him. We often discuss my son and his daughter, especially when he has some sort of turmoil that he can't seem to wrap his head around. Every time, our conversations seem to steer toward our insecurities, social issues, plans, and expectations that seem to subconsciously drive our emotions. Every time, our conversations seem to help him. Of course, my friend isn't in a constant state of crisis, and his bad days are few and far between. But when he is struggling, I'm there to help. For that, we're both grateful.

The emotional problems faced by parents of special needs children are no different than those faced by any other parent, but it's a little like raising a child in a fish bowl. The problems are more frequent, loom larger, and overlap until they become too difficult to solve easily. When it builds into a state of perpetual crisis, the discipline of daily reviews, awkward conversations, sacrifice and service might not seem so drastic. It's better than the alternative.

Before my son's autism began to manifest, I felt much like my friend. I was raised in a good home by good parents, and I was fairly confident that I was ready to follow their example. I was successful and confident with strong opinions about parenting. I believed it was important to be honest and straightforward. I believed that people should strive to be loving and unselfish. For the most part, I lived up to these ideals. I was young, ambitious, and eager to start a family. My future looked good, and I was fairly satisfied with my life choices.

All of that began to change as my son's problems began to appear. His speech came slowly. His interactions were limited. He excelled with all of the physical milestones, but he was slow to develop behaviorally. Worry and anxiety began to replace any confidence that I had in the beginning, and frequent tantrums and meltdowns began to chip away at my sanity. Fears about my future and my son's multiplied with every delay, and that began to change my personality, little by little. Soon, the strain began to show. I was frequently angry, filled with fear, and struggling with every relationship from work acquaintances to friends and family.

This was a difficult time for my son and for me. Tantrums and meltdowns were common. He would scratch and fight. His screaming fits began to dominate our lives. Soon, my son's struggles began to preoccupy me. I couldn't focus on anything else, and my life began to unravel. I couldn't focus on work. I couldn't focus on other members of the family, my friends, or even my spouse. Feelings of helplessness and inadequacy consumed me, and I began to get more protective and controlling as fear began to motivate me. By the time I realized that I was in crisis, I was probably the last to know.

My feelings about parenting hadn't changed. I still felt that a parent should be honest, straightforward, loving, and selfless, but I was finding it more and more impossible to live up to those ideals. On the other hand, fear and insecurity had warped my perspective so much that it was impossible for me to see my actions from anybody else's perspective. Even when somebody pointed out my tendencies to be controlling, manipulative, demanding, or selfish, I could easily justify my actions. I had become so focused on defending and promoting my son and myself that I had lost all perspective of the world around me. That is the real problem faced by a parent of a special needs child, and it is isolating.

Today, I've become grateful for that day at the youth baseball tournament and the ordeal that followed. It marked a low point in my battle against my son's special needs. No parent likes to admit that they feel so negatively toward their own child—angry, hateful, and defiant—but that's the way I felt sitting on my coffee table with my head in my hands, hoping that the police would come to take him away. That's when I was finally able to see the truth. I was in crisis, too. The way I clawed myself out of that crisis was drastic but necessary.

First, I had to understand the crisis. This took a level of self-evaluation and meditation that few parents need, but it was necessary to gain a proper perspective on my emotional turmoil and the way it fueled my own behavior. This isn't unique to special needs parents. I've come across many parents who, locked in a warped perspective, exploded into a problem like a wrecking ball, creating more problems than solutions.

During my sports writing days, I encountered more than one group of parents with a vendetta against a coach, and I've seen them act in embarrassing ways as they try to manipulate the situation to get their way rather than mentoring their children through the challenges of a personality conflict. I can't help but wonder how many lessons were lost or the price that was paid later on in life when those children found themselves in a similar situation, with an ineffective boss or a challenging neighbor. Did they have the tools to be successful despite the circumstances? Had they learned to find peace and purpose in a world that isn't always fair? I hope so.

We've all heard tales about a parent storming into a school to defend their child against a "bad" teacher, and the same questions arise. Did the child learn that they can be successful even if they don't get their way? When I hear about road rage sparked by another driver in traffic, I can't help but wonder if the lesson was lost. Did the justified anger lead to a better coping skill? Was there any self-evaluation that helped the person learn that peacefulness is possible even if our security is threatened? Is the impact of our reaction to an injustice more harmful than the injustice itself? Does the punishment fit the crime? Not always.

This is the ultimate advantage to raising a special needs child. All parents face fears about their children's futures. All children face unique challenges, delays, and difficult stages, but a special needs family encounters these situations on a daily basis. They face more obstacles, and every solution is complicated by unique challenges. Special needs children have more insecurities, greater social challenges, and so many obstacles to their success that emotions run higher, fears run deeper, and anger is always at the fingertips of any caring parent. Most parents can survive a bad day, a stress-filled week, or a few challenging months, but a special needs parent can become overwhelmed by the sheer volume of challenges that they face. Most parents can afford to drop the ball every now and then. A special needs parent doesn't have that luxury. An angry outburst or a panic-fueled spree can have lasting repercussions for the parent and the child. When failures pile up, crisis is imminent.

For a parent in crisis, changing their perspective is not a luxury but a matter of survival. No matter how strong the conviction to be honest, straightforward, loving, and selfless, a parent in crisis will find it impossible to live up to our ideals when driven by wildly erratic emotions. A parent in crisis will find life to be a confusing problem that isn't easily solved. But, if that same parent learns to discover the underlying cause for their crisis, they might be able to find peace and purpose despite their chaotic lives. It may prove to be simpler than any other solution. Instead of focusing all of our efforts on defending ourselves and our children from the everyday threats, obstacles, and social vulnerabilities, we can learn to overcome them. We can develop a consistent approach to an overwhelming situation, and it can pay off.

For me, it all started with a daily review. As I reviewed those moments of crisis in my life that were sparked by security issues, I was finally able to address them. Over time, I was able to easily identify issues that most people take for granted, and I developed better coping mechanisms for my many insecurities. Eventually, those financial issues didn't scare me as much as they did before, and I wasn't consumed by safety and security issues. Sure, my son's meltdowns often turned physical, but I found that I could calmly deal with his outbursts even when I felt physically threatened. We began to venture out into public confidently when I stopped trying to control our environment. Since I was no longer burning energy erratically, I found myself better able to address those community issues and political insecurities that used to overwhelm me. As I became more aware of the conscious and unconscious threats that we face each day, they no longer had the power to overlap, grow, and drive me toward crisis. When vulnerabilities are identified early, proactive solutions are easier to implement, and that state of crisis can be averted.

Special needs families struggle more than most people to overcome social barriers, and that can easily throw a person out of balance. Language and communication issues can overwhelm parents and children. Inclusion issues only serve to reinforce isolation and loneliness. Once these basic issues are overcome, those ordinary challenges of fitting into society are often complicated by special needs. Normal issues of pride, self-esteem, social standing, ego, and importance can be challenging to a family already dealing with inclusion issues. Often relationships suffer. Friendship and romance can be just as tricky for special needs children as it is for their parents. Understanding social issues is crucial in order to develop healthy strategies and coping mechanisms. With early intervention, social crisis can be averted, and we can learn to develop healthy relationships and social circles.

Moments of crisis are often sparked by obstacles to our plans, expectations, schedules, and routines. Nothing can warp our perspective quicker than an unrealistic goal that fails or a situation where we aren't getting our way. The need for accommodations or modifications can drive any special needs parent to develop complex schemes and detailed designs for living that can place unreasonable demands on ourselves and the world around us. Nothing can spark a crisis easier than an unexpected obstacle or unfairness that leads to an unsuccessful plan. Despite good intentions, a parent can become controlling, manipulative, unloving, and selfish. Unhealthy ambition sets in motion a chain of circumstances that leads to a crisis. If we become consciously aware of threats to our ambitions, we can avoid an unconscious reaction if things don't go our way.

All people face insecurities, social problems, and everyday challenges to our plans. All children must learn ways to overcome obstacles, and all parents must find ways to help them overcome their problems. In this way, special needs parents are no different than anyone else. If we can get past our unique challenges and obstacles, we can find that we are not as different as it might feel. As we learn to discuss those problems with security, society, and success, we will find common ground with others whether they understand our children's special needs or not. Sharing our problems and solutions with others can finally give us the sense of purpose and direction that so many special needs parents crave. Open communication with others will help us find solutions that work, and breaking down our walls will finally end the isolation and loneliness that we so often feel.

Nobody is powerful enough to eliminate all of life's threats, obstacles and vulnerabilities, but learning to live with them is the key to a useful and meaningful existence. Sacrifice and service is the pathway. Once a parent in crisis learns to sacrifice the unreasonable demands that we make on ourselves, our children, and society, we can focus on mentoring our children past their own securities to build healthy relationships and a successful life.

Through our experiences, we can help our children understand their feelings before a crisis erupts. We can help them to cope with their insecurities. We can partner with them to improve their social skills, and we can assist them in overcoming mistakes and interruptions. If a parent can overcome their own crisis, that experience will be the best tool for assisting their special needs child. We will finally be able to grow together with our children, mentoring them through major milestones like love, death, and puberty through our own experiences and coping skills.

With this new perspective, we finally reengage with the world around us. We learn to get along with others, starting with those closest to us. Through self-evaluation, communication, and service, I was able to overcome the dysfunction of a broken marriage, and devote myself to co-parenting a special needs child. I became less interested in our differences and more committed to cooperation. I learned better ways to handle different parenting styles and different personalities. I developed more effective skills for avoiding conflicts over power dynamics, and I learned to disregard those problems that didn't concern me. It took commitment and practice, but the effort was definitely worth it. Eventually, I learned to apply those skills at my son's school, with my peers, and even with strangers. As my relationship with the world improved, those negative emotions no longer ruled me. My patience and tolerance grew, and I found that my relationship with my son better prepared me for relating to everyone else in the world. I became less interested in getting my way, more interested in other people and their problems, and more secure in myself.

Once we find peace and purpose, all sorts of remarkable things happen. I've been able to share my experiences with families in those early stages of learning to live with a child with special needs. As a parent of a special needs adult, I have been approached by many parents, family members, or friends who might be coming to terms with a special needs loved one. I enjoy that relieved look that comes when they realize that someone understands. Being able to put those moments of crisis into words, along with my understanding of the causes, the conditions, and the solutions I've found, almost makes it worth the struggle our family went through. There is no better feeling than watching someone shrug off their crisis and embrace a life of peace, purpose, and self-realization.

Like every family, we still have our problems. But we have become more secure—physically, mentally, and emotionally. We've become less anxious about the future and more engaged in our community. We still have financial concerns, but they don't seem to dominate us like they used to. There are still many issues that we face, and we sometimes face a new and unexpected emotional crisis. But we are usually able to find peace, even when we are insecure. We've learned to celebrate our small successes instead of waiting for the other shoe to drop.

Socially, we've improved. In many ways, there's an advantage to having a special needs child. He helps filter relationships, but that allows us to develop those that do exist. Self-awareness has helped us to avoid unreasonable expectations and become more flexible. Consequently, we have learned to grow meaningful relationships and develop good, lasting friendships. Even romance is possible. By solving our emotional crisis, marriages can be strengthened and single parents can find partnerships that work.

Most importantly, opportunities to be useful present themselves in interesting ways. People take notice when they encounter a special needs parent with an understanding of their emotional issues and a solution that works. Friends, family, and acquaintances often refer loved ones to us, especially those struggling with special needs. Often, it's like looking into a mirror. It's easy to spot the fatigue, the helicopter parenting, the self-esteem issues that are prevalent in a special needs home.

Finding a parent who has solved these problems is like striking gold. We can offer a lifeline. We can listen with an understanding ear. Sometimes, these awkward encounters lead to lasting friendships. We live in an era that is fortunate to have a wealth of support groups, special needs communities, and community programs that seemed impossible to earlier generations. It's becoming easier to meet like-minded people who understand and support us. The whole world is opening up to special needs children and their families.

The best news we can offer to a parent who is struggling to come to terms with their family's special needs is that peace and purpose are possible. Parenting a special needs child offered me a unique and meaningful opportunity to grow, help another person, and get out of the way. It is wonderful to be able to celebrate small victories that go unnoticed in most families, to recognize strengths in others, and welcome their assistance. My son is the most fascinating person I have ever met, and it is a privilege to be a part of his development. I have met many special needs parents who feel the same way.

There are many decisions that special needs parents must consider that are outside the scope of this book. Questions arise about medicating our children, incorporating religious opinions and practices, or developing different parenting styles. Everyone has to answer these questions for themselves, but no matter which path we choose, our decisions will be more honest and straightforward, less selfish, and more loving if we are able to avoid crisis to find peace and purpose. If we can solve our emotional crisis, we find that we can make wiser, more rational decisions, and we are better able to handle the results whether it goes our way or not.

Similar to every parent, there are no pat answers or all-encompassing solutions that fit every instance. We all have to find a way that works for us and our families based on our own beliefs and unique circumstances. There are a number of different styles that parents employ when raising a special needs child. I leaned into an acceptance of my son's condition, acknowledging symptoms that created obstacles, and devoting our resources to living peacefully with those condition. I didn't allow him to use his condition as an excuse not to try new things, but we settled comfortably into lives outside of the mainstream. Our unique household was almost sculpted by his condition, but we found unique ways to enjoy daily living and build a solid social circle. Our co-parenting schedules, vacation arrangements, and the family's financial situation might not appeal to other families, but it doesn't have to. Parents of special needs children adopt all sorts of living situations in the same way that every household develops its own culture.

I have known parents who devote themselves to teaching, transforming their homes into amazing learning environments. Their activities center on hands-on learning, and their projects are always designed for building skills. Often their children excel in ways that surprise family and friends, achieving success that defies expert predictions. These parents are disciplined, consistent, and filled with purpose. Tell this parent that their child cannot do something, and watch them prove you wrong. Their children often develop into confident adults who work well within society.

There are also parents who devote themselves to overcoming their child's conditions. They familiarize themselves with every groundbreaking study. At IEP meetings, they are often better qualified than any of the specialists at the table. They are determined and creative. They often adopt new and exciting ways to address issues. They become pioneers in the educational field or clinical experts for the treatment of their children's condition. They amaze family and friends with their boundless energy. These are the ones who change the world.

Many fine parents commit themselves to advocacy. Their ultimate aim is a normal life for their child. They fight for services. They champion their child's rights and work toward creative solutions. These are the parents who fight for inclusion, forcing local school systems to find ways to include special needs children in the classroom. They are active in the school community. Often, they spearhead campaigns for clubs and extracurricular activities. They organize public events and descend on government meetings. Try to tell these parents that their child can't do something, and they'll force you to reconsider your thinking. They will break barriers and bring awareness to the struggles and success of special needs children. These parents are the ones who local newspapers seek because they advocate, not only for their child, but for all others in the community.

Often, different parents adopt different styles, and that diversity is a great strength in the special needs community. I know a family who survived divorce and separation. The mother is a fierce advocate for her child, while the father devotes his time and energy to the peace of the home. Their child has blossomed under this teamwork, and their child has developed a personality that complements both of her parents. As a duo, the parents always seem to be in complete step with one another and in perfect harmony with their child. When the mother turns her attention to a cause, the father sweeps in to nurture. Their ability to support one another is extraordinary, and their effort pays off.

Of course, there are many separated families who are able to work together when it comes to their children. I am reminded of another family I know that has developed such a great "good cop, bad cop" routine that they are a formidable opponent for any unsuspecting administrator. They advocate so strongly as a pair that they have been able to open doors for their child that once seemed impossible. They are like a pair of caged tigers once the gate swings open, and there is no cause that seems to slow them down. They are absolutely in lockstep with each other. It may be surprising to learn that their child is confident and sweet. There isn't a hint of fight within him, and he's a joy to be around. That's because his parental team has created a safe and nurturing environment in the home that contradicts their no-holds-barred attitude outside the home, and they did it despite separation and divorce.

There is no right or wrong when it comes to parenting styles. Every parental approach can reap great benefits for the child and the community, and every approach has its drawbacks. But, if parenting is approached in a sane, healthy manner, parents can find purpose and meaning that will change their lives for the better. With two healthy parents, any child will blossom and mature in confidence, ability and independence. Much of a child's success lies outside a parent's control, but if the parent is honest and straightforward, loving, and unselfish, the child will flourish. Every parent wants their children to reach their potential, and special needs parents are no different. Consistency and stability are the keys.

No matter what style a parent embraces, there is no way to avoid the emotional roller coaster that sometimes plagues the family during a child's development. In that way, special needs families are no different than any other family. Overcoming emotions is crucial if a parent is going to be successful. If a parent is committed to creating a peaceful environment, there is no place for crisis or tantrums. If education and development are the parents' main objectives, then they need to avoid frustration or worry. The same can be said for those parents who work so diligently to find answers and treatment for a child's condition. Emotion-fueled advocates are rarely successful if they are unable to treat others with respect or if their arguments devolve into tantrums or emotional pleas. In any parental style, unbridled emotions can be booby traps that hinder success.

In all cases, parents are most effective if they can learn to spot and avoid those moments of crisis. Developing the discipline to identify those moments, along with the persistence to uncover their causes and conditions, is critical. Learning ways to overcome those underlying conditions puts us in a position to mentor our children. Learning to communicate honestly and lovingly is important, whether it be with a spouse, a co-parent, a teacher, or a child who's struggling. A unified front helps to build healthy teams at home, at school, and in the community. When emotional issues are overcome, great things happen for the family and the child. That's the purpose of this book.

Decisions are always easier when emotions are in check, and that is so important with special needs children. Parents of special needs children are often forced to make all sorts of decisions that most parents will never need to consider, and the ramifications of these decisions can affect the whole family for years to come.

Parents of special needs children will often confront difficult decisions about medications and treatment. These decisions should be made thoughtfully and carefully. Should a child be medicated? Should that continue indefinitely or is it a temporary solution? These decisions, by their very nature, are emotional. They are better considered when not fueled by anger, fear, or confusion. They should be made after consulting with a doctor or expert and should consider the parent's opinions, any religious and scientific beliefs, along with the child's individual needs. Everyone must make the choice that's right for their family and their unique situation. That requires a clear head, an open mind, and a thorough discussion.

Some parents must make grueling decisions that no one should be forced to make. Perhaps their special needs child would be better served in an institution or a group home. Perhaps, because of their condition or unique needs, it is unsafe or unwise for a child to live with the parent. Once again, this decision must be made with all factors considered since it will affect the parents, the child, and every other member of the family. Plans, routines, security, and relationships will be affected, and that can drive all sorts of emotional responses. Understanding the feelings of guilt, fear, or hurt, along with the underlying causes, will help to make better, clear-minded decisions for your child and your family. Understanding ourselves can help us to build strong relationships with our children even if our living conditions are unconventional.

Finally, we find that all parents are alike in many ways. We all want our children to live, thrive, and gain as much independence as they can. If we can get out of ourselves, we are better able to see that all parents face insecurity at times. All parents struggle with relationships and ambitions. We begin to see how similar we are no matter what our unique circumstances turn out to be and whether are children have special needs or not.

All children, at times, face an obstacle or hurdle that seems too big to handle. Every parent, at times, feels ill-equipped to help. No man is an island unto himself. We see our children's frustration as they face their personal crisis, but we don't always know how to help. Everybody needs assistance at times, but knowing when and how is always a challenge. As parents, we are well prepared to recognize our child's limitations, especially if we can recognize our own. We may want to help them, but we don't always know where to begin. Sometimes, we can force solutions that create more problems than we ever intended. We often find ourselves in conflict with the very people we're trying to help.

But, if we've solved similar problems in our own lives, we are in a better position to help our children through their problems by being honest about our own challenges, as thorough as possible with our understanding of ourselves, and as lovingly as possible when we talk about our successes and failures. Whether it's a physical, emotional, mental, or social problem, all parents can benefit from self-evaluation and crafting ideals, but most of us won't need to or want to commit to such a drastic solution of inventory and action.

In a special needs home, drastic measures are often the only solution. How frequently do our children's problems go unnoticed? Our solutions often fall on deaf ears. We often struggle together in the same home, miles apart emotionally from the ones we love the most. This is the greatest challenge for the parent with a special needs child. It is unavoidable. It can be overwhelming. It often dominates our lives.

A friend once told me that if anybody realized what it took to be a parent, nobody would choose to do it. I disagree. Parenting offers great benefits. It broadens our perspective, offers opportunities for unconditional love, and gives a purpose beyond ourselves. Sure, at times, most parents feel ill-equipped for the challenge. After all, being responsible for another human being is a tremendous commitment. There will be many successes and frequent failures, good days and challenging ones. To love unconditionally, to be honest in words and deed, and to sacrifice oneself for another can be monumental tasks. In fact, perfect parenting is an unattainable ideal, but it's the journey that matters. At least it was in our family.

It's been more than a decade since our home was overrun by frequent outbursts, chronic anxiety, and constant confusion. Over the years, my son and I have become much better at understanding our emotions, and we've found solutions that work for both of us. Much like other families, our lives ebb and flow, but we've been able to build consistent relationships with the world around us that aren't driven by conflict and competition. My son has a healthy relationship with both of his parents, along with his extended family and a small community of friends. Although my son continues to struggle with his language skills, his emotional and physical maturity has exceeded every expectation. His special needs can still complicate daily living, but we've learned to face challenges head-on with some measure of grace and dignity.

Along the way, we've found that there is a silver lining to living in a special needs home. There's a freedom from that drive for success, money, and prestige that often dominates the modern world. Our lives have adopted a simpler pace that allows us to smell the roses. Without the competition that drives many in our society, we have become free to appreciate the success of others. We've been able to develop relationships with our family and friends that seem elusive to many in a world that moves so quickly.

Our lives aren't always easy. We sometimes experience setbacks, and progress can often come at an interminably slow pace, but in a very real way, my son and I have grown up together. Because of his condition, we were forced to develop a disciplined approach to our emotions that most people would never attempt, but it has led to a life without crisis, a deep understanding of my strengths and weaknesses, and a commitment to sacrifice and service that has given all of us a sense of peace and purpose.

I still end most days with a careful review of my emotional well-being. It is rare to encounter moments of crisis that were once so common in those early days, but my inventories still uncover emotional problems that go unnoticed by most people. There's always room for improvement. Hardly a day goes by where I can't find an emotionally charged moment if I look hard enough. I still feel anger, but it rarely erupts into a tantrum. I still harbor fear, but it seldom keeps me up at night. Feelings no longer drive or paralyze my decisions because I've learned to recognize their causes and address them before they become critical. I've developed healthy coping mechanisms, and practiced being honest and straightforward, unselfish and loving—even when I'm feeling threatened or hurt.

My life is no longer in crisis, and the same can be said for my son. If we can do it, you can, too.

# ABOUT THE AUTHOR

John E. Goralski is an award-winning journalist and photographer, an editor, a publisher, and the father of a special needs child. He resides in Connecticut with his son, Jack.

John began his writing career after the birth of his son, who was diagnosed with autism as a toddler in the early 2000s. Prior to this, he had been working in the insurance industry after graduating from the University of Connecticut in 1991 with a degree in English.

His career shift was necessitated by his son's diagnosis, so that he could earn a living while also having the flexibility to become the primary caregiver for his special needs child. The next two decades would provide an arduous and challenging journey of understanding and learning how to deal with the many levels of crisis, stemming from the many insecurities, social issues, and obstacles that are so prevalent in special needs homes. He overcame the challenges of divorce, poverty, and isolation that pervades the special needs home.

John's unique ability to combine his real-life experience and education with introspective thought-analysis, helps provide a smart and creative road map for living a peaceful and purpose-driven life despite the inevitable emotional hazards that special needs parents face.

Whether you have a special needs family member or are struggling to handle any other difficult life situation, this book will open your eyes to a new way of thinking. Inevitably, you will learn to better navigate your own unique challenges to find a sense of peace and purpose no matter what your situation.

# ABOUT THE COVER

I had just purchased my first digital camera to use as a journalist, and I was setting it up on my front porch while my eight-year-old wandered around the front yard. I clicked the zoom lens into position, whirled the camera to my face, and zoomed in on my son before pressing the shutter button.

*Chicka-chicka-chicka-chick.* The camera clicked off seven pictures per second as my son played in the yard. After a few seconds I let up on the shutter, but it wasn't until I pulled the pictures up on my computer that I realized what I had captured. I paged through the photos one by one until one captured my attention. *My son was staring directly into the camera!*

The picture floored me. At this stage of his development, everyone was working on his eye contact. At best, he could manage to hold someone's gaze for a second, but that would require so much effort that his face would be twisted up in agony. But here, during this one accidental shutter click, his eye contact looked natural and focused. I printed a copy and hung it on my wall where it still holds a prominent position at eye level...if you're kneeling on the floor.

Whenever we were playing or interacting on the floor, and I was getting frustrated about his lack of eye contact...I'd steal a glance at the photo on the wall. Any parent of an autistic child will understand this. That one photo, captured by mistake in a series of test shots, proved to be the most treasured one I've ever owned. It has been a big source of comfort so many times.

Some critics may argue that a tormented child, yelling red-faced at the camera, might have been a better option as the cover of a book called "Parent in Crisis," but I disagree. In my opinion, there's no better image about finding peace in a special needs home than the one that hangs on my wall. This book is about overcoming *my* crisis, not his, and no picture captures that feeling of peace and purpose than this one.

www.ingramcontent.com/pod-product-compliance
Lightning Source LLC
Chambersburg PA
CBHW010655060526
44119CB00093B/431/J